UPLIFT
BOOK 1

JANET GROOM

Copyright © 2020 Janet Groom
ISBN 978-1-9160997-9-1 (Print)

UPLIFT - Book 1

First Edition
Published by ALP House Publishing
www.alphousepublishing.com

All rights reserved.

No part of this book may be reproduced by any mechanical, photographic or electronic process, or in the form of a phonographic recording, nor may it be stored in a retrieval system, transmitted or otherwise be copied for public or private use, without prior written permission of the publisher and/or author.

Cover image by eommina from Pixabay.com

DISCLAIMER

The contents of this book are purely based on the personal insights and views of the contributors. They are offered in the spirit to share and support, however, in no way are any of the suggestions contained within meant to replace advice from a medical professional where required.

During these extenuating times, please follow advice provided by your Government and Healthcare Professionals.

CONTENTS

The UPLIFT 2020 Project	11
Love Letter to Uplift the World	17
A Walk on The Beach	23
Change Your Mind, Change Your State	27
The Owl, The Ant and The Tree	33
The Joys of Lists	37
Letter of Hope to the World	45
Poem — Rainbow Ella	51
Love of Life	53
The UPLIFT Technique	61
Ten Life Lessons from Lockdown	69
Poem — Shoe Leather Wine	75
The Healing Power of Nature	77
Top Ten Tips to Surviving Lockdown	79
Isolation Haikus	81
Journeying into Hope and Gratitude	85
A Time to Heal	87
Poem — The Tomatoes of Hope and Love	95
Stress Relief at your Fingertips	97
Love is…	103
Children of a Lesser Parent	113
Happiness and Gratitude	121
Pandemic and Haikus	123
Poem — The Way of Life	125
Poem — If It's Me	129
Ten Ways to Bring Joy into Your Days	132
Letter to the World from Mother Nature	136
Survival Tools	144
From Busy to Being	150

Acknowledgments	161
Contributors	165
Join the The UPLIFT 2020 Project	171
Janet Groom - Founder of The UPLIFT 2020 Project	173
ALP House Publishing	175

DEDICATIONS

*To all our **Frontline Heroes**, from our healthcare professionals to our shop workers, our postage staff, teachers, delivery and transport staff, refuse collectors and those who each play their part in saving lives, keeping us safe and providing us with what we need.*

---

*A special mention to **Colonel Tom Moore**, who in the days in the lead up to his 100th birthday, showed the world that one person truly can make a difference raising millions to support the NHS.*

You are a HERO to inspire us all.

'Superhuman'

*Street art painted by Catman
(Whitstable, Kent, UK)*

THE UPLIFT 2020 PROJECT

The UPLIFT 2020 Project has been founded with the aim to provide encouragement and support to people, near and far.

Right across the world our lives changed overnight and being forced into lockdown has been as a vital step in the effort to save lives. However, for us, as human beings, this has been difficult for many. We are designed to be sociable and thrive in communities.

STAY AT HOME
KEEP SAFE
SAVE LIVES

This **UPLIFT Book** is a collection of short inspirational stories, poems, tip lists, coaching tools, as well as artwork — submitted by people from Kent, the UK and across the World.

All proceeds from the sale of this book
will go to support these UK-based charities:

NHSCharitiesTogether.co.uk
Mind.org.uk
Porchlight.org.uk

DONATE >>> www.justgiving.com/crowdfunding/uplift-2020

RAISING SPIRITS is vital at this time. Reaching out, across the divide, to support one another. It is heartwarming to read of the daily acts of kindness being shown to neighbours, to strangers and to support other countries.

> *Together we help raise each other up by offering the hand of kindness.*

LOVE is another part of the UPLIFT formula. It is so much more than a word to bandy around, it is a deep emotion, a connection with oneself and the world around us. It is the bond from which stems compassion, kindness, joy and unity. It is the bridge that brings us together. It is the core of each one of us.

 The authentic essence of love is our guiding light.

All too often people look for love in the world around them — searching for it in material belongings, climbing career ladders, or in the arms of another. The truth is that LOVE is within us all. Those who find it and tune into it shift the perspective on life and see the world in a new way.

 Love is the salve to heal the pain.

Many of the stories show that even in our darkest hour there is still hope and love is the key to heal your pain and unlock the door to your happiness.

By finding our own way to our true love within, we find the path to connecting and enjoying our lives in a deeper way. We see the beauty in the world and in each other.

HOPE is the tiny glimmer of light in the darkness guiding us safely home. We always have hope, and for many, it is the lifeline to help keep our head above the water. Right now we need hope, we need to believe that all will be well. It is this hope that keeps us afloat in these challenging times. As we fix our sights firmly on following hope, it guides us and as we get nearer, the light intensifies until we step out of the darkness.

Let us come together and show that as ONE we have the power to change the world.

JOIN US over on Facebook at the UPLIFT Hub
https://www.facebook.com/groups/UPLIFTHub

SUBSCRIBE and follow us on YouTube
https://www.youtube.com/channel/UCFjpzip0fm9R23EzALc8Nvg

FREE GIFTS FOR YOU

Click here to claim your FREE gifts for purchasing the book - courses, handouts, free discovery sessions, a book and more…
www.janetgroom.com/upliftbookfreebies/

UPLIFT

To Raise or Elevate Emotionally & Spiritually

LOVE LETTER TO UPLIFT THE WORLD

CHANNELLED BY CAROLINE PALMY (SWITZERLAND)

Dear Beautiful Soul,

You are amazing, yes you are.

Don't you believe me, OK, let's look back, look back over your left shoulder, remember how far you have come. Remember all the challenges you've mastered, remember all the smiles you shared. Now it is time to give yourself a pat on your back. You have come such a long way, and you are doing great. Now, again, you are amazing, please remember always.

You are beautiful, oh yes you are.

You are beautiful inside and out, when you smile the world uplifts and cheers for you. Imagine yourself as a flower, what colour would you be, what kind of flower would you be, who (in flower form) would be around you. Now look at yourself, your unique beauty. You are a beautiful flower, so keep on shining gorgeous one.

You are gorgeous

Remember that one time you assisted someone, when you did a good deed, and remember how that person looked at you with gratitude. The world was smiling at you and seeing you in all your gorgeousness. So today you are asked to do something just for yourself. How can you help yourself today?

You are a shining star

Deep at night, when the sky is dark, you are the star that shines and sparkles. Even during the day, when the sun shines the brightest you also shine and sparkle, though you might not see it as clearly as at night. Keep shining beautiful star.

You are an inspiration

Remember that time when you helped a friend, when you maybe shared some of your wisdom or insights. Do you remember how that friend was inspired? Go within, remember what your friend did next, how did your inspiration help them?

You are incredible

I know sometimes you felt the mountains were just too high, and still you made it all the way to the top. Sometimes you felt the valleys were too dark and yet again you made it through. You are incredible and we clap our hands and bow our heads.

You are outstanding

If we were asked to put a grade on you, we could honestly say A+, you are doing a fabulous job. Whatever you were called to do, you did outstandingly. You are helping mankind in your own unique way and you are helping uplift the energy of Mother Earth, whether you realise it or not. Keep doing what you are doing, you are outstanding.

You are awe inspiring

There are days, when you take our breath away. There are days you are so awe inspiring it brings tears to our eyes. We are so fond of you always, and we love how resilient you are, and how you keep going, and we know you believe in yourself if only with an inkling sometimes, though that is all that is ever needed. Never let that spark dull. Keep us in awe dear one.

And sometimes you are only human after all

We feel for you, truly, and we are so proud how you learn to be human, how humbled you feel. How you deal with duality of your everyday life. How you brace yourself for the roller coaster of ups and downs. It is ok to cry; it is OK to feel discouraged and it is OK to not be OK. We love how you embrace it all, and how you make the best of every day. You are a beautiful human being, and we thank you for this.

You are supported

We are always right by your side. We are cheering you on, when life feels a bit hard. We support you on your good days and support you on your not so good days. Sometimes you might feel lonely, though we are right there with you. Expand your energy, expand your body, and feel us right there with you, always.

You are so loved

We love you; we always have and we always will. We know you have forgotten that you are loved. You might have looked far and wide for love, and only when you started to look within you found that love in your heart. When you feel your heart beat, remember this is a sign from us to you, that we love you deeply. With every breath you take, breathe in the love and breathe out all your doubts and worries and fears. You are a vessel of love and we love you deeply, now take a deep breath in and remember that you are truly and deeply loved always.

We are so proud of you

> Warmest of hugs and much love
> The Universe

Caroline Palmy

Caroline is an award winning Author, Speaker and Heart Flow Healer. She helps gorgeous Empaths, Sensitive Souls, Earth Angels and Giving hearts to come back into the flow of love.

Caroline cannot help but express and embody her heart, and helps other to find express and embody their hearts too. She teaches from the heart for the heart and of the heart.

Her first book *Conversations With Me* was published July 2018, and won a mention on Janey Loves Platinum Award List. Her second book *Loving Conversations With Me* was published on 6 May 2019, and went on the bestseller list.

She lives in Switzerland, with her three young adult kids, a golden retriever, a cat and nine tortoises, surrounded by nature.

Contact Caroline at www.carolinepalmy.com

"The Journey is listening to your own inner voice."

-- *Sue Allsworth*
www.authenticsmile.com

A WALK ON THE BEACH

LISA NEWMAN (KENT, UK)

I walked along the empty beach. The sea was calm, the air bright blue, with whispery slivers of white cloud that looked hand painted across the sky. I could see the outline of Calais and felt like waving in case someone over there could see me.

'Sunset by the Sea' photo by Janet Groom

A day like today at any other time would be thriving with bodies. A long line at the ice cream van. Beach balls floating back and forth. The smell of sun cream making everyone feel like they were on their summer holiday, even though it was the beginning of April, no inkling of the traditional showers.

I took a deep breath, taking in the view. Knowing I couldn't linger, I had to walk back up the hill to the confines of my home, just let this one moment stand still.

Let this be a normal day, a normal moment. Any other day, we would buy some chips and sit on the stones, watching the people splash around in the sea. Maybe we would go to the pub, get a pint, and sit on a bench outside and chat idly to others whiling away their afternoon.

Those normal days, I took for granted. We all did. The hours that we would spend staring at our phones, mindlessly scrolling. Searching through Netflix for an hour before watching a film I had seen before, just because I thought there was nothing better to do.

When I could have been outside, going anywhere I wanted. I could have gone for walks with friends. I could have arranged days out with my nieces and nephews. I could have visited my parents, just to have a cup of tea and a chat. Even just going to the shops to buy a healthy lunch, now instead digging out the final pizza from the back of the freezer because going to the supermarket is a mission.

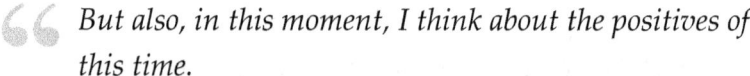
But also, in this moment, I think about the positives of this time.

My house is spotless. My home office has become my place of sanity — it's where I write about my worries and fears, it's where I have purpose. My whole world is currently contained within my house, and so I have learnt where to find tranquillity, where to be productive, where to find comfort.

Being healthy is a different concept than what it was a month ago. Before it was being the fittest, the strongest. Now being healthy means getting a bit of fresh air every day. It means finding ways to get my limbs moving and my heart rate up in the small square of my living room. It means getting on the phone and laughing with my friends and family every day.

I feel more connected to people. My friends and I constantly exchange memes throughout the day, trying to make light of the situation and blame everything on some TV celebrity. We have pub quizzes online on Friday nights, and get drunk in our pyjamas. I have conversations with my mum's curtains and my dad's forehead, because they still haven't quite managed to angle their phones right. But this doesn't just apply to my loved ones, it applies to strangers. Everyone I meet on those rare occasions out of the house, talk to on business calls, interact with on social media, we all have something to talk about. Every person has bonded over this shared, strange experience.

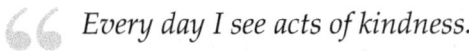 *Every day I see acts of kindness.*

I arrived at the Age UK centre to fill in a volunteer application form and find there was a queue of people wanting to do their bit. On a Thursday evening, everyone in my cul-de-sac stands on their driveway to clap, bang pots and pans, one family with sparklers. We heard the clapping echoing in the neighbouring streets. And a childhood friend leaves a packet of Bakewell tarts on my doorstep when she knows I have had a tough day.

* Life will never be the same again after this, but maybe that is not a bad thing.

* People are constantly looking for ways to be kind and look out for one another.

* Basic hygiene is at the forefront of everyone's mind.

* We have learnt how easy it has been for us to get everything we need, and to recognise those things that, as it turns out, we can easily live without.

* We are more aware how much we depend on interactions with our friends and family.

* We know how important fresh air and basic freedom is essential for our mental well-being.

These things, we will never take for granted again.

CHANGE YOUR MIND, CHANGE YOUR STATE

SHARON LYNN (KENT, UK)

How often do you get frustrated, angry, depressed or tense? Wouldn't it be great if you could always feel fulfilled, calm, joyous and relaxed?

Well you can - and it's actually pretty simple to do!

Firstly, you must realise that everything you feel is because you are choosing to feel that way. You might initially disagree; I know I did when I first heard this. So, read that again, and let it sink in. *The way you feel is your choice!* Yes, someone might do or say something that makes you angry, but how you choose to feel about that long-term is entirely up to you. I now choose to only experience a 'yukky' emotion for just a few moments, before I turn it into something better. So how can you do the same? Simple...

Change your mind about how you are feeling, and you can change your state. Go back and look at the first question at the top. It mentions 'yukky' feelings like frustration, anger, depression, and tension. Now look at the second question; there you are asked to imagine feeling fulfilled, calm, joyous and relaxed - the opposite of the initial feelings, right? So, when you start to feel something that doesn't feel good to you, ask yourself the following:

"If I could stop feeling 'this',
what would I like to be feeling instead?"

Or you could ask

"What is the opposite of what I am currently feeling?"

So, here's some examples of words or feelings that don't feel so great (aka **Shadow**) and words that would be a great choice to switch with (aka **Light**).

Shadow feeling		Light state
Confusion	change to	Clarity
Fear	change to	Love
Fatigue	change to	Vitality
Lack	change to	Abundance
Stagnation	change to	Flow
Oppression	change to	Freedom
Pessimism	change to	Optimism
Grief	change to	Acceptance

If you look at each of these pairings and really try to feel how each one feels you will realise that you cannot experience one at the same time as the other. It is impossible to be confused and have clarity at the same time. It's also impossible to feel fear at the same time as having the most gorgeous experience of unconditional love (like when hugging a loved one or pet for example). They just don't vibrate at the same level and therefore cannot co-exist.

So next time you feel a 'shadow' thought or feeling popping in - STOP - then flick an imaginary switch in your brain that gets you to come up with the opposite of that unhelpful thought or feeling and start saying, and feeling, that 'light' emotion instead.

"Change your mind, change your state!"

SHIFTING YOUR STATE WITH AFFIRMATIONS

Taking the previous exercise one step further, you can now create some positive Affirmations (with your 'light' words) which will help you to shift your state even further. This will allow you to experience positive feelings and states of being whenever you choose. For most words you can simply place 'I am' in front, for example - *"I Am Acceptance. I Am Flow. I Am Clarity. I Am Abundance"*.

It might seem a little weird at first saying things like *"I Am Abundance"* (as opposed to I Am Abundant or I Am enjoying Abundance), but I have found this slight shift in how you state your " I Am's" makes a difference.

So, try to state the word you want i.e. Abundance, because by doing this you become the vibration of Abundance and it therefore becomes your experience. In whichever way you choose to create your Affirmations, they must always be in the 'now' as if it already is your experience.

AFFIRMATION

"As I watch this transition with fascination & curiosity, I realise... I am eternal"

www.MysticMouse-Publishing.com

Once you've got the hang of simple one word "I Am" statements, then you can start to create other Affirmations with more than one 'light' word together. You can then have fun creating even longer, more specific, powerful, and positive, present based ones. Once you have created one or two 'state changers' that really resonate with how you would like to feel or be, say them every day for 30 days (as that's how long it is suggested the subconscious mind takes to create a new neural pathway and belief). Then see how much better things feel in a month's time!

Just a few more examples to inspire your own personalised Affirmations:

"I Am Calm, I Am Joy and I Am loving life"
"I choose Peace, Harmony & Love"
"I enjoy a Happy, Rewarding life full of Vitality"
"As I Surrender into Gratitude and Acceptance,
I experience Peace"
"I embrace New Beginnings with Strength & Wisdom"
"I Am Love. I Am in Love. I Am of Love and I exude Love"
"Every cell in my body is Rejuvenating & Regenerating. I feel
Energised and Totally Alive"
"I Am. I just Am; and everything just Is"

These exercises don't only assist you in shining a 'light' on your emotional & mental 'shadows' but they can also help you reach a state of spiritual harmony and oneness with yourself and the 'outside world'. If created and stated correctly they can also improve your physical health & overall well-being beyond recognition. Affirmations literally saved me.

"My path is clear and I move forward in a purposeful & positive way"

Finally, if you are feeling even more creative why not find some inspiring images as a backdrop for what you come up with.

May you see in yourself what I see in you. May you believe in yourself as I believe in you.

Many Blessings...

Sharon Lynn

Sharon is a highly Intuitive Soul, Starseed and Transformational Facilitator. She is a Vibrational & Multi-Dimensional Healer and has been connecting to, and channeling wisdom from, 'things unseen' since 1998. She also follows a 'Shamanic Way', observing and listening to the messages of anything (but particularly animals) that comes her way.

She is the founder of The Entrepreneurial Lightworker and Mystic Mouse Publishing. As a Speaker, Author, Creative and Workshop Leader her purpose is to share wisdom and enlighten & inspire others in being the best vibration they can BE; thus raising the vibration of the planet through LOVE.

Contact Sharon at www.MysticMouse-Publishing.com

THE OWL, THE ANT AND THE TREE

JANET GROOM (KENT, UK)

A tale for young and old with a message for us all. So, sit down, read carefully and listen. *Once upon a time…*

An owl was sitting on the branch,
Surveying the world below
And thinking.
That's what owls do.
They are known for their wisdom,
The wise old owl.

Far below, a tiny Ant.
An industrious creature,
Was working away.
Carrying food back to its colony,
To feed the Queen
And all the other ants.

"You are worthless tiny ant",
Said the Owl,
Spotting the little creature,
On the ground below.
"You are not wise like me,
You do not have wisdom.
You are nothing."

The tiny Ant stopped in her tracks
And stared up high into the branches above.
She saw the Owl looking down at her.
She sat down her heavy load,
Thought for a moment and replied,
"I am small, but I work hard.
I can carry twenty times my own weight.
I work hard to provide for my Queen,
And my colony family."

THE OWL, THE ANT AND THE TREE

The Owl sat for a moment,
And then answered.
"Yes, but you are not clever like me,
I have been granted the wisdom
Of my forefathers.
I know more than you ever will
And think beyond your comprehension."

The Ant studied the Owl,
And replied.
"Perhaps, this is true,
But wisdom does not feed us,
It is our work that gets
Things done."

Before the Owl could answer,
There came from deep within the Tree
A sigh, that made the leaves rustle,
As the old oak Tree woke up.

"Ah, my children, listen…
You are both God's children.
You each have your role.
Like the Sun,
Who greets each new day -
And the Moon,
Who watches over us each night.

We must all honour,
And respect each other.
We are ONE,

We are all part of Nature,
Do not forget."

The Tree went back to sleep.
The Owl went back to thinking.
And the tiny Ant went back to work.

Since that day, and every day
The Owl would nod in greeting
To the Ant,
The Ant would nod back to the Owl.
And they both bowed to the Tree.

THE JOYS OF LISTS

EMMA DEVEREUX (KENT, UK)

I've never done anything by halves, and I've always thought to myself that if I'm going to be busy doing something, I may as well be really busy doing everything! I've always worked — through school, university and teacher training, then when I got there, I still decided one job wasn't enough and became a WW coach too. I enjoy being busy, I thrive on structure. I enjoy a project and love to have a sense of purpose whenever I take anything on. When I have too much time on my hands, I, like many other people I meet and coach, make poor choices when it comes to maintaining my physical and mental health and well-being. The "I'll do it later" mentality starts to creep in, especially when I am not accountable to anybody else. In my day-to-day life I juggle a lot; deadlines, data, meetings, appointments as well the human element that comes with both of my chosen vocations. While this keeps me focussed and accountable, it doesn't leave me with a lot of time to make poor choices with food, activity or self-care. I have a strong routine and I find this is what helps me stay positive and make good choices.

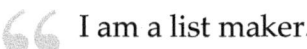 I am a list maker.

I love a list, of any kind. A shopping list, a to-do list, a list of films I want to watch or songs I want to listen to, Christmas and Birthday lists, lists of things I'd like to try, bucket lists, lists of things I'm grateful for… the list goes on! I make a list and, naturally, I want to tick off whatever is on there. During this global pandemic, I have had more time on my hands than I can ever remember, but lists have been my saviour. A list keeps me accountable; it gives me a purpose and it helps me to keep in some sort of routine. Not long, sprawling lists of completely inspired tasks, but functional lists of things I would like to have accomplished by the end of the day or week. Naturally though, with all of this time on my hands, a simple handwritten list was not enough for me. I took up bullet journaling. I wanted to make my lists look lovely, because then I would enjoy creating them, and I would enjoy re-visiting them and also, it was a task in itself - something to work on and something to do. On any given day I would strive for 3 'basics', these were: one thing to achieve, one thing for me and one connection — EVERY day. Then on any given week I would add in more things, but at the bare minimum, it would include the three basics. This added structure and purpose to an endless stream of days where there was seemingly nothing to do and no obvious purpose. After creating these weekly spreads in my journal, I also realised I would have something really positive to look back on once life returned to normal. I would be able to reflect on all the positive changes and choices I had made, how productive I had been, and how much I had grown as a person.

Once my basic list had been created, I would set to work achieving the tasks I'd set myself, and that got me thinking. What if I encouraged others to complete my tasks with me? What if I could incorporate my connections into another project? What if I could do things for me which also benefitted another area of my life, or contributed to my personal growth or skill set? All of a sudden, my days started to fill up with meaningful connections, learning new skills, working on projects, doing all of those 'I'll do it later' jobs. I was finding that my days during lockdown were busy and full of purpose. My lists evolved and I would separate my weeks into my basic categories, I would create a weekly spread with *seven* ideas in each category, this gave me an element of choice. I was finding that I would have to turn down, or re-schedule virtual events because my days had become so packed with meaningful tasks and connections, I had almost forgotten that I was even on lockdown in the first place.

If list-making is not your cup of tea, and you are not a organised thinker or a creative type, don't let it stop you. Find something that works for you, find your own way of creating purpose. You can use all of the principles without physically putting anything down on paper. You can still achieve all the basic tasks without having to log it in any particular way. It is the practice of physically doing something meaningful that will boost your mood, your well-being, your health and your happiness. If you're struggling to even think of productive things to do in the absence of your normal routine, that's fine too. Look online, make connections and ask others how they are passing their time, join virtual groups and interact with other members. Or at the very least, have a look at some of the examples included below. Above all, it's important to be kind to yourself, to cut yourself some slack occasionally. The world has never known anything like this, and everybody can be forgiven for finding it tough. Speak to yourself how you would speak to a friend, show yourself the same compassion. The things that you can control are your words, your actions and what you put out into the world. Focus on making those things the best that they can be, and the rest will come.

Something to achieve
Do the hoovering
Do a load of laundry
Change the bed sheets
Clean a bathroom
Do the food shopping
Cook a meal
Bake a cake
Catch up on sorting your finances
Clear out a cluttered cupboard
Sort out and donate unwanted clothes
Work on tasks for your job from home
Put up the pictures you never got around to hanging
Wash the car
Do the dishes

Something for you
Read a book
Learn another language
Paint or draw a picture
Learn to draw
Learn calligraphy
Do an exercise class (DVD or virtual)
Start running
Go on a long walk

Create a gratitude journal
Make a photo album
Listen to music
Pamper yourself — paint your nails, slap on a face mask, have a long bath
Meditate
Watch your favourite film or TV programme

Make Connections
Video call friends and family
Live-stream your favourite music
Join virtual groups and become part of a community
Have a 'virtual games night'
Make time for 'Date Night' at home
Send an old-fashioned letter
Speak to your neighbours
Get involved with online classes
Leave a lovely message on a YouTube video or Instagram post - let's build people up
Take part in a virtual pub quiz
Set your family and friends challenges and share the results
Suggest a socially distanced street party
Start a blog or YouTube channel
Offer up your skills to help others

I'm sorry
Please forgive me
I thank you
I love you

— Ho'oponopono Prayer

GRATITUDE

With my eyes I can see,
all there is grateful to be.
With my ears I can hear,
choosing gratitude and not fear.
With my nose I can smell,
making my heart oh so swell.
With my hands I can touch,
all that I am blessed with so much.
With my tongue I can taste,
let's make sure we leave no waste.
With my heart I can feel,
that my life is now the real deal.
With my heart I can be Grateful
to the God
who's inside of me.

-- Sue Allsworth
www.authenticsmile.com

LETTER OF HOPE TO THE WORLD

ANGELA BRITTAIN (TEXAS, USA)

Hope
Kindness
Compassion
Love

April 13, 2020
Easter

Dear World

The sun came up again today, as it always has for us, and I have faith it will rise again tomorrow. Faith is often described as belief in the unknown, faith in the unseen. The sun came up as normal, but not much else in the world this day feels normal. The world is experiencing a global pandemic that has taken the lives of over a million people. Yet I still have faith to believe it will eventually be alright and maybe even better despite the death and illness we see all around the world.

There are many reasons to have faith and the HOPE it brings. We see people reaching out in kindness to help others like we have never seen before. Stories abound that are so beautiful and filled with sharing and caring that you can't help but have hope.

Neighbours helping neighbours they have never met. People are now reaching out to strangers to offer help. A bond is being built.

People are beginning to recognise the small things in life we have always taken for granted and we now find a new sense of appreciation for those things and each other. Parents are forced to stay home with their children and are playing games and doing puzzles together. These will be fond memories for the children and will overshadow the turmoil of the pandemic.

People who have always rushed through their days on autopilot without really seeing the world around them are now forced to slow down and even stop the rushing about. We are learning who we are inside ourselves. We have become more introspective.

The movie stars and athletes we have idolised for so many years have been mostly replaced by ordinary people such as grocery cashiers, stockers, firemen and women, police officers and especially the courageous medical professionals risking their own lives to treat the sick. These are now the ones we see as the heroes that we admire and applaud. Oh, and the store stocker who keeps the toilet paper on the shelves in our time of need.

Pollution of air and water have seen a dramatic decrease. One report had CO_2 levels in major cities dropping by over 18%. The canals in Venice are clear, the air over major cities are no longer grey with smog, blue skies have returned, and people are looking up and smiling as they search for cloud formations that resemble animals. Playing the game with our children, it reminds us of when we were children and felt such glee as we found rabbits and elephants in the clouds.

Rivalling drug gangs in Africa who used to steal and terrorise their neighbourhoods have come together and stopped fighting. And in a peaceful, caring gesture they are taking food and medicine into the neighbourhoods they once terrorised and even giving money to the impoverished areas. The rivalling gangs are now working together for the good of the local people. We can hope this will continue.

In these unprecedented times that we witness in the world, we see people are mostly being kind to strangers, people they will never meet, but feel compassion for them and feel a need to do any small act to help. Donating money or volunteering their time to work in the food banks and distribute food to so many unemployed people who are struggling to feed their families.

Yes, the pandemic has physically separated us, locked us away in our homes, but it has brought us together emotionally and spiritually as we awaken to the reality that we are indeed a global community. We are seeing the commonalities we share and those commonalities far out-number any differences we may have.

May we enter into a more peaceful and loving world. May we not forget the lessons we learn in these times of social distance but stay focused on the hope for a better future.

Have faith. Have HOPE.

With much Love always
Hope

Angela Brittain

Angela is a Certified Dream Builder Coach, whose heart-centred approach can help you overcome your fears and design a life that's in harmony with your Soul's purpose.

For over 25 years Angela has worked with small business entrepreneurs, as well as individuals helping them build their dreams, accelerate their results, and create richer, more fulfilling lives.

Angela is the author of the book *You Can't Love Him into Loving You*, and she also is a co-author in Brian Tracy's book *Cracking the Code to Success*.

Contact Angela at www.angelabrittainllc.com

I AM ME

I am Me.

Who else can I be?

I am Love.
I am Joy.
I am Light.

I am Free
When I embrace me,
In my entirety

I am Me.

— Ellie J. Hart

POEM — RAINBOW ELLA

HAYLEY KENNETT (KENT, UK)

Rainbow Ella, Rainbow Ella
What joy you bring us, Rainbow Ella
Your striking colours are so bold
We look forward to chasing your pot of gold.

In the darkest days your colours shine
Telling us all that in the end, it'll all be fine
Yes there are days that make us feel blue
But we can't give up as we have our jobs to do.

When your arches emblazon the sky it's true
You can see all the colours,
Red, orange, yellow, green, violet, indigo and blue
Those colours make us feel fuzzy, happy and hopeful
Your presence in the sky is just so beautiful.

Archie Reynolds, aged 12
Faverhsam, Kent, UK

Rainbow Ella, Rainbow Ella
What joy you bring us, Rainbow Ella
Thank for appearing in the sky, continually gifting
You are truly amazing, unique and uplifting.

LOVE OF LIFE

SUSANNE MUELLER (NEW YORK, USA)

Love of life – it is the very little moments that count.

We are all so super busy being inundated with stuff and information that we cannot see or explore the tiny, precious moments in life. A wake-up call is necessary. How do you want to be woken up, gently? Take a step forward and learn to enjoy your precious life moments.

My love of life is running.

To many people running means a lot of work, endurance, determination, and training endless hours: yes, it is all of the above and more. However, it also creates for me the little, treasured moments that I need in my life. As a busy New Yorker, moments of being super quiet are required and necessary if not mandatory. You might wonder how? OK the city that never sleeps takes a lot of energy out of me. I am overwhelmed with the offerings that this city provides, I am getting sucked into that high energy and fast and high drive. Have you ever been to New York? If you are a good observer, New Yorkers walk faster, they talk faster — it's all about time. New Yorkers do not have that much time, time is money for them. Then how can you escape from that as a sensitive person and not been overrun or burnt out?

While it is super cool to be out and about all the time that takes tons of energy. I love to be involved in art, in music, and in my field of expertise of organisational development, coaching, leadership and women's leadership - or just namely learning and networking: then this is truly the best place to be. OK, but if you are tired and exhausted from all those events you are not really effective, productive, nor successful.

What I have implemented is my own policy of attending one event per week, so I do not get over-excited with too much. Believe me, this has saved me in the long run.

**In order to stay healthy and sane,
my outlet is the running.**

For that I am following a training plan. The plan allows me to keep a balance: think, I cannot run every day, this would not be healthy and sustainable. I have to date completed 26 marathon distance races, 1 ironman triathlon distance and climbed Mt. Kilimanjaro. I know from the mountaineering mantra *'go slow in order to go fast'* that this is the way to be. So, this means that while training for long distance races, I need to find my balance between enough and too much. My body usually tells me when it is too much — I get exhausted and I feel sick. I need to rest up much more — from an Olympic 5km distance runner, I learned that resting is part of the training. Nobody should go from not running at all to running a marathon — this would not be very wise.

Then how can the running be my love of life?

Running is more than just putting on my shoes and entering the park to run a few kilometres. To me it is about my quiet time, my me-time, my feel-good time, and mostly my freedom — running unites us.

Quiet time: yes, I do not run with music — I am probably one of the few people who gets distracted while listening to music. I like to listen to my surroundings — and yes, even in New York's Central Park you can hear the birds. It is the green lung of New York; it is where I can rejuvenate and recharge my batteries fully.

Me-time: like many busy people, this is the only time that I take out for me. This is the time when nobody can talk to me. This is MY time. As an executive coach, I see many times that this me-time is overlooked. You want to be of service to all, you want to be of service at all times. This is actually a wrong approach. In order to be of service to others, you need to rejuvenate and recharge the batteries on a very regular basis. Remember what they say in the airplane? *'Put the oxygen mask first on you and then on others.'* Makes sense? Do you remember the last time you took some time for yourself? It is worth putting it into your calendar. I have me-time in my calendar carved out as *Meeting with the CEO*. I am the CEO of my company and I am also the driver of my own life. I need my running, hence during the week, I use my lunchtime as my running time. This is my lunch meeting with me.

My feel-good time: nothing is better to me when I am running and the wind is blowing through my hair. These are the times when I feel the best. It is creating the flow of running. I feel good and I cannot explain why, totally. Do you ever have a feeling like that? I feel like I am on top of things, I feel I can conquer anything — I am in my element. The running makes me stronger; the running makes me tougher and more prepared for whatever is ahead of me. In difficult times, I like to run more — maybe not speed and long distances, but I like to feel good when times are challenging.

My freedom: running provides pure freedom. I can run whenever I want, I can run wherever I am. Running is a great past-time that can be performed anywhere around the world. I know there are some restrictions in some cultures but that does not hinder me from practicing it. I remember I was visiting the island of Borneo in Indonesia. In the hotel there was a gym. I watched who went to the gym and at what time. I realised that mostly it was men and no women. After a while, I checked out the gym and asked if I could run there as well. The answer was: "YES, why not." I covered myself up with a long skirt to walk to the gym and then changed into my shorts. Just walking on the premises of the hotels in shorts would have made me too uncomfortable as I wanted to respect the local culture. I felt at ease running in the gym with other people there — both men and women.

Running unites: whenever I add *marathon running* into my resume/CV, this has been the topic that was of interest for an easy discussion. If you have a passion and dedication that you love, let the world know of it. Anyone who is a runner, short or longer distances, will have great and inspirational stories. Everybody must start somewhere; never forget how strong that bond is.

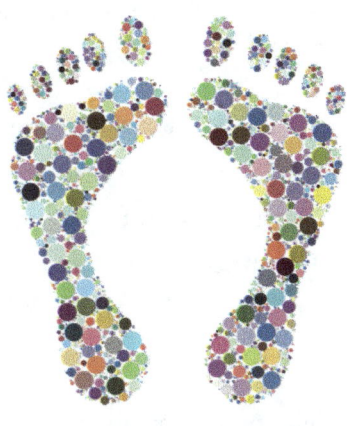

Historically, running was for men only. Women had to conquer the sports while signing up for races as men. So, the running trend and development can be compared to women's leadership. Women have to fight to be accepted in the world. Now, in today's races the majority of participants are women. The statistics have changed — this is a positive development. I am proud of that and also proud that I can be part of this movement.

Each step I take while running counts for me, I am proud of all my medals for my many races I have participated in. Participation counts as much as the winning. Remember, we all start at the same place and we all cross the finish line at the same place, just in different time orders. Not everybody can be a winner — but we are all *winners of life*.

Nobody can take running and the freedom it gives away from me. Every step is a little moment that I count and cherish tremendously.

Susanne Mueller

Susanne is originally from Switzerland, residing in New York. She has an MA in Organisational Development & Leadership, a BA in Psychology, and an Executive Coaching Certificate from Columbia University.

In her global career, she worked for Swiss airlines, the Swiss Mission to the United Nations, and Nestlé in the Global Human Resources department. She is a facilitator for mindfulness group coaching and has coached leaders globally in 60+ countries. She is a certified running coach, a triathlete (full Ironman distance), marathon runner, and yogini — and climbed Mt. Kilimanjaro.

Susanne is a published author, weekly blogger and podcaster. Contact Susanne at www.susannemueller.biz

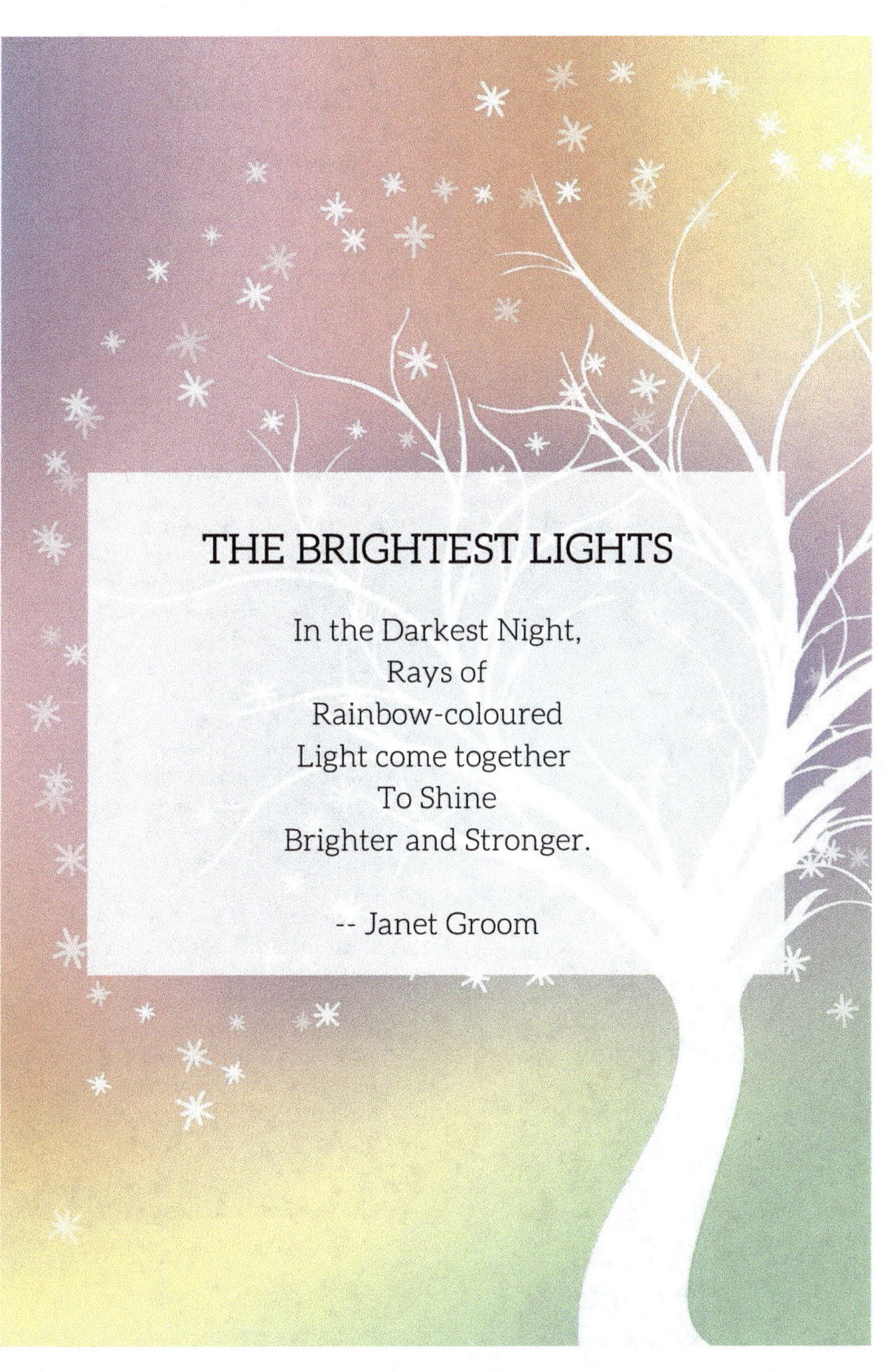

The Vagabond

Give to me the life I love,
Let the lave go by me,
Give the jolly heaven above
And the byway night me.
Bed in the bush with stars to see,
Bread I dip in the river --
There's the life for a man like me,
There's the life for ever.

Let the blow fall soon or late,
Let what will be o'er me;
Give the face of earth around
And the road before me.
Wealth I seek not, hope nor love,
Nor a friend to know me;
All I seek, the heaven above
And the road below me.

Or let autumn fall on me
Where afield I linger,
Silencing the bird on tree,
Biting the blue finger;
White as meal the frosty field --
Warm the fireside haven --
Not to autumn will I yield,
Not to winter even!

Let the blow fall soon or late,
Let what will be o'er me;
Give the face of earth around,
And the road before me.
Wealth I ask not, hope, nor love,
Nor a friend to know me.
All I ask, the heaven above
And the road below me.

-- Robert Louis Stevenson

The favourite poem
of
Mrs Eileen Reid
Tandragree, Northern Ireland

THE UPLIFT TECHNIQUE

JANE SCANLAN (BOURNEMOUTH, UK)

My names Jane Scanlan, I help stressed mums in business get clear, calm and confident to live their uplifted lives, by using Confidence Coaching and Holistic Therapies.

I would like to share with you my process I personally use and guide clients through to get Clear, Calm and Confident, to live their Uplifted Lives!

Over the past 10 years I have transformed my life from one I really wasn't happy with but unconsciously created through chaos, to a life I love and have consciously created by getting clear, calm and confident. Let me take you through the step by step process, the deeper you dive, the deeper your transformation.

Grab a journal, a pen, and a drink — it's time to start.

Let's Uplift Our Lives, and the ripple effect will Uplift the World.

The UPLIFT Technique

1. **Be Willing to Change**
Write down all the ways and areas in your life that you are willing to change.

2. **The Art of Knowing**
Write a list of all the things you aren't happy with in your life. As the saying goes it's better out than in!
i. I hate …
ii. I'm worried …
iii. I dislike …
iv. I'm afraid …
v. I don't want …

Flip each of those 'perceived negatives' into what you truly desire, this will help you create your uplifted life.
i. I hate my 9 – 5 office job
ii. Flip into = I run a XYZ business I love, work X hours a week, and earn X a month

3. **Learn to Let Go**
Write the limiting beliefs that you hold about yourself, others, the world, and your transformation.
It's time to give your belief system an upgrade!
Now, write down your upgraded beliefs about yourself, others,

the world and your transformation. These could become part of your self-love routine or gratitude practice, see steps 5 and 6.

i. I am depressed/down/low

ii. I focus on joy, love and laughter to uplift my life!

Photo Credit: 'Weston Super Mare' Pete Stanley of Pete's Photography www.petesphotography.net

4. Dare to Dream

Your dream doesn't need to be filled with private jets if that's not your thing…fill your uplifted life vision with all the things that are important to you! Look at step 3 to help visualise your dream and then write out 'Your Perfect Day', in the present tense, as if you are living your uplifted life right now.

5. Love You

Self-love will uplift you like nothing else. What self-love routines could you start implementing in your life?

6. An Attitude of Gratitude

If you desire a full and complete uplifted life transformation an

Attitude of Gratitude is required? Write down 5 things you are grateful for, and do this every day.

7. **Be the Change**
Your uplifted life transformation will only happen if you do the work, feel the feelings and implement what you say you're going to do. How can you be the change you want to see in the world today? What is your next step?

I am so pleased you've taken the time to work through these steps to uplift your life. Please share your uplifted life transformation with us, share The UPLIFT Technique with your friends and the world!

Jane Scanlan

Jane Scanlan is "The Queen of Making It Simple" and helps stressed mums in business get clear, calm and confident in all areas of their lives and businesses. She uses her Life Coaching online courses, Confidence Coaching Sessions and Holistic Therapies to help the mind, body and soul to align with all her membership clients.

She boasts more than 15 years of experience within the health and wellness industry, her memberships are some of the best in her local area (bases in

Dorset and London), and globally via online platforms. She has become an Amazon Self Help Best Selling Co-Author with Voices of Hope, received business awards from BHStar Awards and SMBN, and has been featured in The Sun Online and Time & Leisure Magazine.

Connect Jane at www.cherishtransformupgrade.com

Emotions

How do your 'autopilot' emotions affect your perception and life experiences?

*Journal Journey
Chakra Cards
by
AuthenticSmile.com*

Face your emotions one step at a time. What emotion overwhelms you the most and how can you safely confront it? Make a list of what you could do and who could support you through this.

For my Journal:
Today I choose to feel free of the emotion...

The Birds Keep Singing

Illustration: 'Beginnings' by Rhiannon Archard (Faversham, Kent, UK)

"Oh, to be in England now that April's there"
and the birds are singing in the sunshine
the flowers are bursting through the winter soil
but, despite appearances we are in an apocalyptic world,
where a deadly virus chokes the lungs of its victims
and yet, the birds keep singing
an ambulance approaches, this time it's in our street,
a neighbour has the virus perhaps?
too close to home!
another soul taken too soon
how can it be that the streets are empty?
the world as we know it in lockdown?
homes are prison cells
and yet, the birds keep singing
while the NHS frontline battles to save those they can
and my garden looks as it should as spring has sprung,
the air so fresh isn't it?
and still, the birds keep singing
nature is waiting for us to come through this
and we will and all will be well
while the birds keep singing

—

April Austen   @moonstonebrightpoetry

* * *

The Serenity Prayer

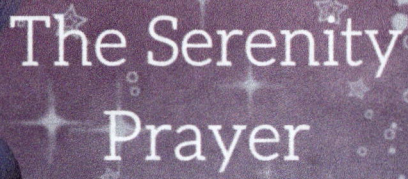

God grant me the
SERENITY
To ACCEPT the things
I cannot CHANGE,
COURAGE
to CHANGE
the things I can,
And the WISDOM
to KNOW the
difference.

TEN LIFE LESSONS FROM LOCKDOWN

FELICITY GRIFFIN CLARK (ROME, ITALY)

Rome, April 2020

The *global pandemic* has turned everything upside down. Our old life feels as remote as the Armada, or the building of the pyramids; and our new life can feel like every disaster movie you've ever seen. So how do we cope when our life is a continuous present and the future is both remote and opaque?

In Rome as I write we are entering Week 7 of complete lockdown. No one is allowed to leave their home unless they are on urgent business: shopping for food or medicines, an urgent medical appointment, a brief dog walk or exercise. No one may be outside without having signed their form swearing they are not sick with the *virus* and that you understand your region's quarantine rules. Police may stop you at any time to ask for your documents. The streets are empty. Only police and army vehicles and the occasional empty bus go past. Drones and helicopters fly low overhead checking the streets for people breaking the lockdown.

But while the regulations feel oppressive and lockdown is not easy, Italians are still friendly and cheerful. We nod and smile and say 'buongiorno' to each other in the street or wave and smile from windows. Flags and homemade banners declaring 'Andrà tutto bene' (everything will be ok) hang from balconies or are taped to front doors.

I grab onto the shreds of community spirit. It is a stronghold back into the past normal where life was busy, the famous 'baci e abbracci' was the way you greeted people and where the future looked rosy. Facing down fear and anxiety is a daily challenge. But we know from history that there are deep and important lessons to be learned from times of hardship.

TEN LIFE LESSONS FROM LOCKDOWN

After many weeks of lockdown in Rome this is what I have learned:

1) Humans are hardwired for connection and will connect even if they have to stay 2 metres apart. In spite of masks and separation, there is kindness and smiling.

2) Buying stuff is over-rated. For so long we have looked for happiness in possessions: a bigger house, a flashier car, disposable fashion and glamorous holidays. But this time has brought home the deep truth that family, friends, our common humanity matter more than anything else.

3) Once humans are taken out of the equation, Nature will reassert itself. From the first week of lockdown my daily dog walk has shown that Nature will rush back fiercely when people are no longer around. Instead of fumes, the air is clean and bright and smells of the country. Instead of traffic noise, there is birdsong. Wildflowers blossom down the Via Fori Imperiali and they are full of bees and butterflies.

4) Art, writing, music, any creative activity will soothe your soul and distract you from anxiety, worry and despair. Losing yourself in your chosen art form is the best way to detach from the continual tide of news.

5) Space and time to just be is vital, and a luxury in our world. We no longer have the excuse that there is no time to think, or that one day you'll get around to practising mediation or writing your novel, or just stopping for a while. How many people are

now baking bread or taking an online course because they have both the time and the inclination?

6) It is important to get off the treadmill of being available, working 24/7, earning more, buying more. Step back and think of what you really want in your life. Busyness crowds out contemplation. The old pressures no longer hold for many of us. What will you replace them with?

7) It's OK to not read the news, to not post on social media, to tune out from the constant chatter. All the world's religions have prized silence as a way of finding true understanding and contentment. It's OK to just be.

8) Being apart from the world is essential to work out who you really are, what your path is, what's important to you. And it's OK not to have a plan, it's OK not to want what the world is telling you is the best, the only way to live.

9) So much of what we take for granted as fixed and immutable is really just a human construct, not tethered in anything but

convention. Weekdays, weekends, holidays, even the accepted meal times are all just things we agree to.

10) In the end, nothing really matters except having enough to get by, and to love and be loved.

This time of lockdown and separation is a watershed, a turning point for everyone. We can no more go back to 'a normal life' than we can be 17 again. A *pandemic* world is a chance to do things differently, to be true to ourselves and to live a better life.

Australian Artist and Writer living in Rome, Italy.

Owner of the Counterweave Art Gallery www.counterweave.com/

Follow Felicity's experience via her Facebook page
www.facebook.com/Lockdown-Letters-living-in-Rome-during-the-quarantine-104852611157027/

Photos courtesy of Felicity Griffin Clark and Poppy taken during their permitted daily walks through the deserted streets of Rome

The Gift

Gifts come in all shapes and sizes,
but these gifts have been nice surprises.

An hour walk in the sun with my kids in tow,
crafting together instead
of using technology - my foe!

Sitting and talking about previous fun
and things we can do when
this year is all done.

The gifts that's been given is the time to heal,
to listen and learn
from the things that we feel.

We look forward to going back to life as it was,
but for the minute
we embrace the gift of time being paused.

-- Lisa Hall
(Kent, UK)

POEM — SHOE LEATHER WINE

NICKY THOMPSON (KENT, UK)

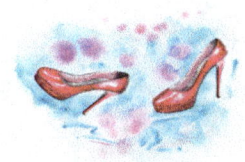

I collect odd shoes, pay pennies
at jumble sales, gather them
from roadsides, the high-tide line.
Old boots, sandals, trainers, lace-ups,
pumps, stilettos. All single.
I lay them side by side by size,
baby's knitted bootie to workman's boot,
see them scuffed and empty.
I reread the recipe, reclassify

by material, fraying fabric, split plastic,
shrivelled leather seasoned with sea salt.
I dissect the animal skin, discard cloth
and metal, broken heels and laces,
pour a gallon of water, stir sugar
and yeast, drop one shoe
after another into the bucket.

The fermenting leather retraces itself.
Escaping bubbles carry away the bitterness

of uphill paths, roads not taken,
lost races, missed goals, unnoticed
first steps and abandoned last dances.
I sip the wine, swallowing summer
holiday sweetness, hopscotch,
skipping, paddling, wading
through waist-high wheat.
I siphon forgotten footsteps
into green glass, saving them
for when I need to just sit.

THE HEALING POWER OF NATURE

HELEN REE (SWITZERLAND)

A s for many, including me, Nature is the best medicine to help bring peace to the mind.

Walks in the forest calm me, and here in Switzerland, a hike in the mountains provides the opportunity to change one's perspective on many levels.

Nature is beautiful, power and valuable to us in many ways — take for example, the humble Fern.

Ferns are a group of plants that can be found all over the world.

 Did you know they are one of the oldest plants growing on earth?

Ferns are not of great economic value, but some may be used for food, medicine and for remediating contaminated soil. And there is research being carried out because of their ability to remove chemical pollutants from the atmosphere.

Photos credit: Copyright (c) Helen Ree www.helenree.com

TOP TEN TIPS TO SURVIVING LOCKDOWN

VIKKI HILLS (KENT, UK)

1) Have a routine (if you can, try to stick to one as close as to your 'normal') — do at least one thing a day at the same time each day.

2) Keep regular contact with at least one person outside your home (not necessarily every day, but whatever works best for you).

3) Have something to look forward to (set up an activity or call with someone in advance).

4) Set yourself realistic goals (give yourself something to work towards achieving every day, big or small).

5) Give yourself space (make sure you fit in some time for just you, we all need a break sometimes — take time out to sit alone with your thoughts without distractions).

6) Do something you love (we need as many moments of joy as we can get — allow yourself time to do something that warms your heart).

7) Use your time wisely (is there something you've been putting off because you couldn't find the time to do it or perhaps you want to learn a new skill? Use this time to do that!).

8) Minimise/stop your engagement with the news (we don't need reminding of all the negative things going on constantly, ask your friends to keep you updated or read into the positive outcomes of this unfortunate event instead — it's not all doom and gloom).

9) Allow yourself to feel sad, anxious, angry — what is happening sucks, and it's OK to acknowledge that, but it doesn't need to consume us.

10) Remember, we are all in this together — this may feel a very lonely time, but we are not alone, the whole world is going through the same thing as us, let's stick together!

ISOLATION HAIKUS

JENNY LUDDINGTON (KENT, UK)

Haiku
a Japanese poem of seventeen syllables, in three lines of five, seven, and five, traditionally evoking images of the natural world.

> Talk, decompression,
> using down time to release,
> process, spring forward.
>
> #allheartled
> #isolationhaikus
> #day10

> Meaningful connection
> with colleague you only know
> peripherally.
>
> #allheartled
> #isolationhaikus
> #day28

> I shall lean deeply
> into the parts that I love
> turn from challenges.
>
> #allheartled
> #isolationhaikus
> #day33

Follow Jenny Luddington's daily Haiku poems
in her Facebook Group *ISOLATION HAIKUS*
www.facebook.com/groups/207577137250149

Psychedelic Flowers
Jane Young
(Kent, UK)

"When something goes wrong in your life,
just shout '*PLOT TWIST*'
and keep moving forward."

-- Sue Allsworth
www.authenticsmile.com

JOURNEYING INTO HOPE AND GRATITUDE

LYDIA HOMER (KENT, UK)

I didn't realise the importance of hope and acting upon hope until I became unwell. I dug deep for hope, wishing and hoping that my very capable consultant was somehow underestimating the healing power of my body.

An acquaintance suggested that if my body had once known how to be well I could call upon my personal 'body blue-print' and find my way back to health.

Instead I decided to create a new blue-print, one filled with hope. Hope to walk unassisted, hope to regain my memory and a full vocabulary, the hope of falling in love, the hope of being and feeling cherished, and the hope of becoming a mother.

It is now 29 years since the beginning of that seed of hope and I have achieved everything on that 'hope list' and considerably more. Sometimes I experienced months of moving forwards with hope in my heart, followed by days, weeks, months, even years of treading water or a sense of drowning.

'Hope' - Heart Filled with Love standing strong with the world, the sunshine lights a present - that is HOPE by Harriet Homer, aged 9 (Kent, UK)

Hope, however, never completely left me, though at times I feared it had. Fortunately, when I quietened my racing thoughts - hope would return. I am grateful for hope. Without hope I would have walked a fearful, lonely path. Hope and taking action has led me to immense gratitude. Hope is the calm that wraps me in a blanket of love.

A TIME TO HEAL

AMANDA HART (SOMERSET, UK)

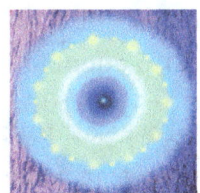

It started with a dry cough. Not often, but enough to make me realise. Four days after doing the weekly shop at the supermarket, a sharp niggle appeared in my only kidney. I thought at first it may be the start of a simple infection, but in hindsight I realise I hadn't worn gloves that day, had been too consumed by the urgency of getting home as it was the only time I could shop for the kids and I, around work. Having stood in the queue for almost two hours waiting to get into the supermarket, my thoughts were on getting the shopping done fast as opposed to how well. Oh, the irony!

So, I rushed in that day, hurtling around, grabbing whatever I could and ignoring the carefully prepared shopping list in my bag and completely forgot my gloves which the kids had made me promise faithfully to wear. By the time I got to the pasta aisle and remembered, it was too late. So, I carried on regardless, my prime focus to get home and start my shift.

In a matter of days, I couldn't believe how wiped out I felt. The kidney by then was painful enough for me to know I had to do something about it. The dilemma was to give me antibiotics to reduce infection, compromising my kidney, that would risk destabilising further an already compromised immune system post recent pleurisy, or I could risk seeing how I got through it. I refused the treatment and made the decision to heal myself instead. Having had meningitis in my thirties, my body was prone to crash, but it was also adept at healing itself.

I got through my shifts that week through thought, prayer and intention. It could not have been a more crucial time at work in community nursing. Whilst I was one of the first wave to work from home, known as the 'engine room' of our organisation coordinating the nurses, my concern was that if I walked away at that point it would compromise stability during a very uncertain time for my clients, the nurses, my colleagues and all the many families associated. My work ethic and conscience battled with my love for my family and my guilt for putting others before myself yet again.

My days had become a consistent rolling out of bed minutes before work, moving to the chair that was inches from my bed and logging on at my dressing table which had become my workspace for the duration of my isolation. No more walks and fresh air in the beautiful surrounding countryside. The four walls of my tiny home, already bursting at the seams with my two grown-up children who'd returned from University armed with all their possessions, already gave me moments of angst but my daily walks had at least been welcome moments of respite.

As the days progressed and symptoms worsened, my four walls were closing in as well as my constricted ability to physically breathe. I knew I had to put my health first if I was going to be able to get back in the saddle to support those I loved and what mattered most. That, I realised, was the only way I was going to truly make a difference.

I felt a tremendous weight of responsibility removed from my shoulders as I not only let go of my full-time role for a while but cancelled all schedules as an author and consultant for the foreseeable future.

Taking on my new role in nursing community care, it had been the family replacement for my children going off to University to alleviate 'empty nest syndrome'. I'd found my surrogate family, but equally the endless juggling of a full-time role, all be it what I loved to do, together with my writing and client work, was creating its own problems with finding the right lifestyle balance that I sorely needed.

As soon as a I let go, I realised that I was still running from past failures and was just too frightened to stop. Success up to then still seemed to be about doing and giving to others but I had neglected to be and give to myself.

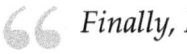 *Finally, I had a choice.*

Several days on after these symptoms began, I sit here in my bed and decide to just give in to this. Guilt makes you do the things that your soul least wants you to do. My head was telling me this morning that I had to get up, go and do 'something', anything that made me feel like I was still operating on all four cylinders but my soul won as I heard my all too familiar angels say *'Today and from now on, you're going to love yourself entirely.'*

It's not easy to let go of a survivor mentality, especially when you've endured so much throughout life and your breaking point is further away than many lead themselves to believe, but it's to those like myself who keep going no matter what that I appeal to at this time. I know there are so many like me out there with that 'British Bulldog' attitude and adversity primed thinking. That works well to a certain degree, but when it comes to putting everyone else first, like me, it may well catch them out when they least expect it. It is not that we need to keep going to the bitter end at times, but it's through understanding our limitations that finally help us realise when to move away from the drama of life in order to find our natural harmony again.

> *Today and from now on, you're going to love yourself entirely.*

In the greater scheme of things, we are all in this together, the whole of humanity. Not even world wars have given us this kind of chance to reflect on overcoming the wrongs and shortcomings we've had to face on such a global scale. This, however, is a time when each and every one of us, rich or poor, old or young, fit or otherwise, religious or not has to face that we're all lumped into this one vast ocean liner going in the same direction.

This is our chance to see if we want to abandon ship and I mean that purely metaphorically. Do we forsake and compromise the promise we made to love ourselves when we came into this world, or do we face this and see where this is taking us, without judgement? That will be hard for many considering what we're witnessing around us with our loved ones, our neighbours and what we face every time we turn our televisions on to see the news.

How can we really move on from this as a human race without being touched by its destruction, its cruelty, its randomness and non-discriminate choice of who's affected? How can we try to make sense of something that seems non-selective and non-compassionate? We can't. So, all we can do is move with the ocean liner that carries us all and honour the journey in the best way we can.

History reveals those such as Martin Luther King, Oprah Winfrey, Maya Angelou and many more that have gone on from adversity to teach the world that love is the only way to create real change and bring us back to a natural state of harmony once more. Despite how we view this right now, there are incredible acts of kindness, compassion for our health services throughout the world, not just the NHS, who are doing whatever they can to love us back.

It is therefore our duty to ourselves and humanity to match that spirit of kindness and give ourselves the very best chance by loving ourselves in order to send that ripple throughout our families, our neighbourhoods, our countries and to the entire world.

Over 50 scientific studies on one particular type of meditation looked into the Maharishi Effect. Meditation has been known through millennia to create powerful transformations for the human soul, having a positively powerful affect mentally, emotionally and physically on us. This study proved that when at least 1% of any given population meditated, it had a knock on affect that increased order and harmony to the entirety of its population and even beyond its borders.

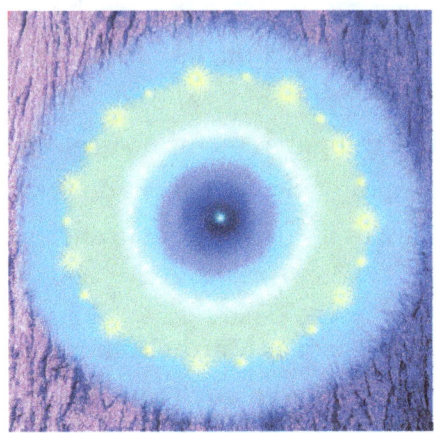

As we're all part of consciousness and as individuals we affect the collective consciousness, in today's world where increased coherence is crucial for our survival, every one of us has the ability to do something every day that will empower and amplify a united worldwide healing through the global consciousness at this time.

This is a time to honour ourselves by taking a moment every day in our own individual way whether that be through prayer, by showing gratitude, saying affirmations or through meditation. Everything you send in that quiet still space of your day is recognised by consciousness and feeds the flame of unconditional love. By honouring your light, you amplify your own and others, connecting with this infinite source of creation to help turn this ship around and help it head to the shores of serenity.

 This is a time to honour ourselves… by honouring our light…

We all have the ability to be resilient, to be resourceful, to have hope and to heal and it is down to our authentic nature that counts when it comes to dealing with the unknown. Only in consciousness is the all-seeing, all knowing, where opportunities and solutions reside, so it's there that we will find our truest ally, our authentic nature and our saving grace.

Whatever you do to make a living, however your situation is right now, you have the power to make a difference for yourself, your loved ones, your community and beyond. It is not for you to judge how consciousness will divvy out your daily intention, it is merely your intention that will define what's best for the greater good of yourself and all…and that's how we'll make this a better world to live in.

Copyright © Amanda Hart, 2020

Amanda is an Intuitive Consultant, who has helped people to overcome negative conditioning for the past 24 years to help them find their power, purpose and voice.

She was a finalist on Britain's Psychic Challenge on TV, a presenter on My Spirit Radio, a columnist for Soul & Spirit Magazine and today writes for Orion Publishing.

Amanda Hart

She is also an author and has written four books and collaborated on four others in the field of wellbeing and speaks publicly about her story, to help others make sense of theirs.

Amanda supports a global audience and works collaboratively with other inspirers from around the world to heal and awaken more souls.

Contact Amanda at www.amanda-hart.co.uk

POEM — THE TOMATOES OF HOPE AND LOVE

JOHNNY HOMER (KENT, UK)

The Tomatoes of Hope (by a man allergic to them)

It is because I love you,
that while clearing the vegetables for the winter to come,
I saved the last tiny tomatoes.
And spared them from the indignity of the compost heap.
I washed them and put them in an earthenware dish,
placed them on the kitchen window ledge
to soak up autumn's dying sun.
Safe in the knowledge the green would turn red,
and that you and Harriet would eat them,
with cheese and some bread,
perhaps some pickles too.

These, surely are the tomatoes of hope and love.

10 NEW THINGS TO TRY

1. Cloud watch - see the different types and shapes and keep a cloud log.
2. Re-read a few of your old favourite books.
3. Discover new music.
4. Stretch yourself - go beyond your usual comfort zones.
5. Find a happy news story and follow up on it and see how it pans out.
6. Indulge in watching some silly television - it's good to laugh.
7. Pick up a pencil and draw a window view or a still life - with no criticism, just enjoy.
8. Learn something new - try a free online course.
9. Keep a diary or journal - noting new daily discoveries.
10. Take a free online Art tour.

-- *Jeanne Ellin,*
Bristol, UK

STRESS RELIEF AT YOUR FINGERTIPS
KARIN HAGELIN (SWITZERLAND)

Right now, many of us are feeling anxious, stressed and overwhelmed about the situation in the world. We are all worried about the wellbeing of our loved ones; about our own mental and physical health, and even about what the future will look like.

It is really challenging to find that inner calm you so desperately need in order to do the practices that normally help, like meditation, yoga and relaxation exercises.

Trust me, I'm in the same boat as you, dear reader.

So what can you do to help yourself handle this overwhelming situation, and find ways to relieve some of that stress and anxiety?

The very weird looking but hugely effective, self-help tool I use to bridge that gap between struggling with emotional turmoil and finding back to a relaxed state is EFT tapping.

Emotional Freedom Techniques (EFT) is a form of meridian tapping that combines the Chinese Medicine acupressure technique and modern psychology with startling results

EFT helps the body's stress response (fight-or-flight response) to re-balance the emotional and hormonal states in the body. By tapping these acupressure points using our fingertips, you are helping your body clear emotional blockages, such as grief, trauma and negative emotions. The memories will be kept intact, but your body does no longer have to react with a physical response when a traumatic memory is recalled or triggered.

You only need to try it out for a couple of minutes and you will notice how the body relaxes. Why don't you give it a go right now?

Let's start by thinking about something that is upsetting you at the moment, or if you are experiencing a physical pain in your body right now. It could be anything from physical pain, irritation, frustration, sadness, worry or the feeling of not being in control over a certain life situation. Notice the feelings or the sensation in your body.

Now imagine a scale from 0-10, where 0 is no pain/no emotional charge and 10 excruciating pain/really upset. Focus on the issue you are experiencing, give it a number between 0-10 and write the number down on a piece of paper.

Start tapping lightly on the side of your hand known as the side of the hand point (see reference video on my website karinhagelin.ch/what-is-eft-tapping/), and breathe. Just tap on the side of the hand, breathe, and notice what happens in your body as you are focusing on the emotional issue or physical pain you chose above.

Now, continue tapping eight to ten times on each point as seen in my reference video, starting with the **eyebrow point**, followed by the **side of eye point, under eye point, under nose point, under mouth point, collarbone point, under arm point**, and end with the **top of head point**, while stating what is going on such as:

"*I have a terrible headache*", "*I'm feeling so anxious*", "*My lower back is killing me*", or "*I'm really fearful and overwhelmed*".

It doesn't matter if you tap on the right or left side of your body, you can also alternate between left and right as you go along. Imagine drumming with your fingers on a tabletop, that's the pressure you should use when tapping on the points.

Remember to focus on the negative feeling first, even if it feels counterintuitive or even a bit scary! The very point of tapping is to give space to the pain or the emotional distress, and not sweep it under the rug and pretend it's not there. It's a lot easier to let go of the emotional or physical pain after it has been properly acknowledged. The point is to address and then release the "bad feelings" instead of pushing them further and further down.

After finishing two rounds of tapping (one round is tapping 8-10 times on each point), take a nice, deep breath.

Now focus on the situation or pain again and see if you can give it a number. How upsetting is it for you to think about it now? How much pain are you in right this moment? Has the number gone up or down?

If it has gone up, continue tapping for a few more rounds until you feel more relaxed. Don't be alarmed if the number goes up after the first one or two rounds; just continue tapping and breathing until you feel more relaxed.

If the number has gone down, check in with yourself and see where your thoughts are now, or how the pain feels now. Continue tapping a few more rounds until you feel calm and grounded. You then do one or two rounds, using statements like:

"I now feel myself relax", *"It is safe for me to let go of the pain"*, or *"Even if the world feels unsafe right now, I choose to feel calm and centred"*.

You can also combine tapping through all the points and stating affirmations such as *"I am well, and the Universe is supporting my journey"*; reciting your favourite prayer or poem; singing or listening to your favourite song; the possibilities are endless!

Close your eyes, take a nice, deep breath, and just scan your body again. Go back to where you started, recall the pain or the emotional state you started tapping on, and do a last check in.

Don't forget to rest and drink a lot of water after using EFT, and remember that you can always come back and do more tapping on the same or similar issues later.

Karin is a Life Crisis Coach helping people manage grief, loss and trauma; get relief from stress and anxiety; release unhealthy patterns of thought and behaviour; and heal relationships.

For more information and resources go to www.karinhagelin.ch

Acceptance

Do you look back with acceptance or do you still hold on to regrets and grudges?

*Journal Journey
Chakra Cards
by
AuthenticSmile.com*

Resisting acceptance is quite often what causes you to feel that you are not in control, as if your power is not your own. Acceptance is a personal feeling within and a choice.

For my Journal:
Today I am ready to accept...
so my life will become...

LOVE IS...

KAVITHA CHAHEL (GLOBAL CITIZEN)

Love is more than saying 'I love you'. Words are so easy to say, yet often hollow and hold nothing in them. Love is much more than a fleeting feeling. It's a feeling that comes from somewhere deep inside and never ever goes away. Let me make a clear distinction here between like and love. I always love my family but believe me there are certain behaviours they exhibit or things they say and do, that I really dislike. It doesn't diminish my love for them. I hope that helps clarify what I am saying when I say that love comes from somewhere stronger than I like you/dislike you. It is fierce, strong and steadfast.

We are bombarded with images that love is something that sweeps you of your feet, and when we don't experience love in that way it's easy to think we don't have love in our life. Love is not one big 'true loves kiss' that somehow miraculously saves you, fills your home with roses and chocolate, and you live happily ever after. Love is far greater than that, far deeper, far more meaningful and sometimes packaged up in negative connotations of duty and responsibility.

There is love in so many small acts that it's easy to not notice the love. My view of what loves means has evolved over the years with the experience of great losses and the associated grief that comes with loss.

My mother sadly passed on the 31st of January 2020. I mourned her while she was alive as I lost her slowly to her very aggressive cancer that consumed her a little day by day. I didn't quite realise just how lucky I had been in my life to have had the mother that I did, until she was gone. She asked me 10 days before she died, 'what have I done right as a mother?' It made me so sad that she even asked me that, because how quick are we in our lives to judge negatively or tell someone when something isn't right. Even to those people whom we love so deeply and so fiercely. I got a chance to tell her what she had done right, what made me smile and the lessons she left with me.

More than my words I got a chance to show her through my actions. Don't get me wrong we fought as mothers and daughters do, we both said some quite cutting things at times and didn't always like each other. By fulfilling my duty and responsibility as a daughter and having mum move in with us once she was diagnosed with cancer, I got to show her that I loved her. I know it is not easy being a carer but we know it is the right thing to do and even in that there is love.

Life will throw curveballs and they can really hurt when they hit. They can knock you straight off your feet. We can be left feeling so vulnerable, alone and afraid. It is then in those moments that love can see us through. For me it was the love and kindness that I was showered with my whole life and after my mum passed away that I feel so much gratitude for. Small acts of kindness and compassion can go much further than you think, just focus on those and that will carry you through when things are hard.

We are in the midst of a global pandemic, the likes of which the world has not seen in over 100 years. It is a really scary time for so many people, how long will things stay like this in limbo before real change happens? How will we survive with no income or very little income? That's not just it, people we know will in this time get sick, some will recover, and others will pass away. People we know and love will also die of causes that are not pandemic related. My father was, a month after my mother passed, diagnosed with small cell lung cancer, which is very aggressive and the consultants have said that he has a matter of a few short months left. I mean you couldn't make this up. Talk about getting knocked off your feet.

Life will continue or discontinue as it always has, and there will be things that trip us up along the way. The metaphorical monsters (or real ones in some cases) always lurk just around the corner. So many of my friends are finding the lockdown that we are all under mentally very taxing.

The thing with all the stress and anxiety that life throws our way is there is always a silver lining, always something to be grateful for. It is that gratitude and love that will see us through. It is the reminder to allow ourselves the feelings of our shadow to show up and really acknowledge those feelings, to then learn how to let those feelings slowly dissipate. To fill the void or emptiness that we may feel, with things that bring light and joy rather than allowing the tentacles of darkness take hold and make its home in our souls.

- What feelings are coming up for you that you need to acknowledge?
- What fills you with joy and light?
- How can you fit more of that into your life?

Like many people on the planet, I have lived through my share of sorrow, grief, disappointment and anger. I have also experienced great love, joy, laughter, gratitude and generosity is so many forms emotional, physical, mental, spiritual and material. And it is a reminder of those moments in my life, that gives me the space to breathe, that brings a smile to my face in times that are heavy and difficult.

What moments have you had in your life that bring a smile to your face?

Here are a few things that I have found that really help uplift my spirits and soul that can be done while we are far away from our loved ones even in the most difficult/challenging times:

1) **Talk to someone**: reach out to a friend, a neighbour, a relative or someone on a helpline; JUST TALK TO SOMEONE. I know that talking does not make the problem go away but just sounding it out with someone can be really helpful. It creates the

space to think about the problem and sometimes see it from a completely different perspective.
- Who will you talk to?
- When will you do this?
- How often do you need to connect?
- Who needs to hear from you?

2) **Set boundaries**: Even in sacrifice and love there has to be boundaries. They keep us safe and let others know what you are comfortable with and what you aren't, so communicate those boundaries clearly.
- Where in your life do you need to set boundaries?
- What are the boundaries?
- How will you communicate them?
- How will you know they are being respected?
- What will you do if they are being violated?
- How will you correct this?

3) **Gratitude**: I cannot stress the importance of this enough. I don't write a gratitude journal daily, or weekly for that matter, so I definitely won't ask you to. I do however practice as much mindfulness as I can each day (I have a toddler that will drag me right into the present regardless of if I am ready to be there or not, so that is helpful). I take time to acknowledge how joyful it is to just even be drawing with my little girl. I have made a habit of being thankful for those moments in my life. I am so grateful we have a roof over our head, food on our table, heating, a hot shower, love, friendship, companionship and laughter. The simple things that are far too easy to just take for granted. I am grateful for the opportunities that my parents created for me through their sacrifice and effort.

- What are you grateful for in your life?
- Who are you grateful for in your life?
- What are you doing to be more mindful in each moment, when your thoughts take you away?

I come back to love; we must begin to love ourselves to really acknowledge love. Know that you deserve love. It's so hard for some people to hear that and even acknowledge that. We are all worthy of love. In the small acts of love and kindness to ourselves and others we not only uplift ourselves through tough times but we can uplift others too.

We can learn to love the *self* even if we don't always like ourselves. Love is deep and unwavering, finding a way out of a difficult situation and learning a new way of being is possible. The world now demands it of us. Economies are being brought to their knees, there is an equalising that needed to happen. The media has fed us lies and fed insecurities, damaging our self-esteem. We are told, each one of us, you are not worthy because you don't live like a billionaire, look like a model, and you aren't a footballer. This list is endless, so much so that we are led to believe if your boobs aren't symmetrical there is something wrong with you, it's ridiculous!

Here is mother nature in her infinite power showing us otherwise. You are worthy of love and real contentment. Contentment is not a destination it is something we carry inside us, like love it has always been there, we just have been too distracted to find it.

Kavitha Chahel

Kavitha Chahel's first book Compassionism, was a finalist at 2016 INDIES Forward Book Awards, in two categories of Business & Economics and Self Help.

Kavitha regularly speaks at events, is a guest lecturer and is an activist for women's rights. She is the non-executive director of a charity that provides safe housing for victims of domestic violence. She has worked with medium sized and fortune 500 companies for over two decades, with clients spread across the globe. She is a leadership coach specialising in Compassionate communication and problem solving

She is a Fellow of the RSA and writes articles for various publications.

Contact Kavitha at www.compassionism.com/

Virtual Hug

Photo Credit: Jitka Kohlickova (Kent, UK)

We open our arms for a virtual hug
and pull each other through this silent fug
friendly faces smile through our screens
and lift our moods as if we'd really seen
the frontline fights to win this new war
with everyone behind them clapping at the door
our arms long to hold our family and friends,
it seems so long until this time ends
but, it will and then we'll party on
and enjoy a coffee mug in a cafes throng
we will pull through into a new world,
we'll start from the beginning
and it'll be gold!

***

April Austen @moonstonebrightpoetry

***

Artwork: 'Luna's Dream'
by Claudia España & Benn Khidhathong

I AM - Power Truths

by
AuthenticSmile.com

Dear World

We really are in this together, as one; simply visualise the bigger picture that The Universe has for you.

WE ARE ONE, from the same energy, there is no separation.

Dear Humanity

This planet of ours is a miracle not to be taken for granted. It is unique. Treat it with respect.

WE ARE all responsible for taking care of the very thing that enables us to live; Earth.

Dear Compassion

Through you I have learned to realise that we are all doing the best we can with what we have.

I AM a better version of myself when I live with compassion in my heart.

CHILDREN OF A LESSER PARENT
JAMES MOFFAT (BERN, SWITZERLAND)

The alarm went off, it was seven o'clock in the morning and I knew it was going to be one of those days. Do I roll over and stay in bed, or do I get up and start the day as normal?

It was actually an easy decision because the children typically come to our bed in the morning and wake us up whether we like it or not, to drag us out for their breakfast.

It wasn't until I was listening to the news later that day, that we learned about the global pandemic and how it was spreading from China across the rest of the world. Basically, with all the news updates and daily statistics of each country being infected, it was only a matter of time before it was 'Coming to a town near you!'

As the virus started to gather momentum, we knew it wouldn't be long before there were some tighter restrictions within

Switzerland. And sure enough, when it did hit, the schools started to close, the shops, the workplace, all events over 1000 people, border controls closing and people stock piling food and for some strange reason, loads of toilet paper.

I was used to working from home, so it didn't really affect me as far as technology and ability to work, as I do have my own home office. Therefore it wasn't going to be a problem, or was it? I hadn't factored in three small children at home 24-hours a day and the impact it would cause. Daily life wasn't going to be the same anymore and we had a whole new set of challenges that we really weren't prepared for.

We never had a plan and we really didn't know what to expect with having home schooling and being teachers, care workers and opening up the house to becoming a huge 'play town'— and was really going to cause a disruption. At first, we kind of made it up as we went along without any plan trying to get through the day, yet this caused more stress, frustration and problems and really didn't work. We, my wife and I, had to come up with a plan, something that would work for all of us and try to bring back some normality in the home.

The home lockdown caught us off guard and we really were not prepared, although after one week of sheer chaos, a ton of stress and disbelief in the whole global situation — we knew we had to do something about it as we were, as parents, going quickly insane.

So much so, the frustration of trying to work and look after kids, the regular home chorus and keeping a safe social distance away from the neighbours and friends, it started to take its toll on all of us, especially the children.

Daddy couldn't be their playmate all day, we were stuck in the house and I had work to do. Yet for them, they didn't really understand being so young, with Tom (7) and Sam and Abi our twins (4). Our home became an 'all-in-one' big school, play area, nursery school, workplace, home and junk shop!

I say junk shop, as my the main task I had was chief house cleaner — even with the help (sometimes) from the kids, it was always a constant mess. To top it all, our eldest son Tom, had been given so much homework from his school, my wife became a full time teacher (although she also has a job and needed to work), which added more stress and annoyance, that the absolute number one priority of our lives was to ensure Tom had his homework done in time. People dying all over the world, but Tom had to have his homework in on time. There was a WhatsApp school class group he had to check into every day, then videos we had to make of his activities, then Zoom calls with his class, his piano lessons online and so on. The stress levels at home became unimaginable.

Although, it didn't finish there, we had Sam and Abi to look after and my constant virtual business calls I tried to sneak off and attend, only to be rudely interrupted by the kids bursting through the door or banging on it for Daddy to come and play.

One week of this was driving me crazy, sitting with kids on my lap on conference calls, in-between playing with them to try and go back to a work mindset afterwards wasn't easy.

The fear is, there is a tipping point and when it happens, it is like a cork exploding out of a shaken champagne bottle and you don't want to be around when it happens. This was me! I couldn't work, was constantly interrupted and I found it extremely hard to concentrate, was easily distracted and leaving my home office to a bomb site in every room added fuel to the fire inside, and a once calm and placid person became a mad man.

It then left me feeling like a bad father and an intolerant husband and I'm hearing myself saying *'children of a lesser parent'* as I really can't cope with this any longer.

So, that was the turning point on formulating a plan.

The plan was pretty straight forward with a bit of trial and error and if it didn't work, make some adjustments. Actually, as part of my business mentoring, I always say you need a plan to my clients, so this is what we did.

As we couldn't change the situation, we could adjust our reality to it and change the way we do things. After all, it wasn't working the way we thought it would and we needed to get our sanity back. A plan that would also benefit the kids and hopefully there would be harmony back in the household.

The days are now split up into manageable time chunks and I

would take the morning shift with the twins, whilst my wife on homework duties with Tom. Depending on the day, we would share the preparation for lunch and only if I had rescheduled calls (between 2-4pm) would I actively do some work. Having set up the technology hurdles for my wife, she was also ready to join her conference calls and we would basically share, as best as possible, the afternoon slot, between work and play.

Then from 5-8pm it was dinner, some more time with the kids and then bedtime, where I could relax a bit with our Interactive Bedtime Story telling. Having mastered this over 4 years, this was the one time I enjoyed and could rekindle the bond with the kids. Starting with Sam & Abi's 'Marvellous Adventures' then when they were asleep, Tom's. This was magical, very interactive, leveraging on their imagination and creativity and we all loved recording yet another story for our long collection.

Around 8.30-9pm it was time to clean up a bit and then I was free!

Free as in, time to start uninterrupted work, without kids bursting in the room, so I could switch back into working mode and catch up on all the things I couldn't do during the day. Like writing this book.

A valuable lesson learnt during the first week, was you can cope with pretty much anything if you work together as a team and have a plan in place. Something simple like a daily wall plan, with a list of activities, including the work plan, just so everyone is on the same page and in agreement with what it is, how it works and each individuals part in this. You can always fine tune it, but only if you have one. Also, look at the things that work, like the **Interactive Bedtime Storytelling** as that is a perfect way to create that calm and much needed bonding that was slightly eroded during the challenging day and a great way to end the day for the kids.

Life is not perfect, we are not perfect, we all have a tipping point, but you can overcome this if you work together as a team.

It's now past midnight, I better finish now and go to bed.

 Goodnight!

Find out about James' Interactive Bedtime Stories at https://en.tipeee.com/interactive-bedtime-storytelling/

James is an entrepreneur, speaker, a meaningful 'WHY' extractor, an interactive bedtime storyteller, and business strategist. Leveraging on more than 20 years of business and life experience, thousands of people have benefited from his comforting sounds as an inspirer. This has helped rediscover, empower and transform the lives of his clients on their business and personal life journeys.

James is originally from Edinburgh, Scotland and now lives in Bern, Switzerland with his wife and 3 young children, where he leverages on their imagination to create very powerful, interactive bedtime stories.

He now shares his experience teaching other parents the Art of Interactive Bedtimes Storytelling.

James Moffat

Contact James at www.facebook.com/jamesmoffat3

The Turtle

Although the journey
may be slow,
We will get
through this.

Ella Austen (Kent, UK)

HAPPINESS AND GRATITUDE

SARAH RICHARDS (LEEDS, UK)

During isolation I have been knitting.

I often knit anyway but I'm now using it as a way of meditating. With each stitch I measure my breathing. With each row I listen to my heart beating.

I'm learning new skills and each time I master a new technique, I celebrate. I celebrate each moment I have with my children. I celebrate my health. Strangely all of this introspection has not made me doubt myself— this is often my reaction to things I cannot control. I feel strong and happy.

Rejoice in what you have.
Take the time to breathe and count your blessings.
You may have more than you thought.

PANDEMIC AND HAIKUS
JITKA KOHLICKOVA (KENT, UK)

Pandemic Survival Haiku

With hope in the best.
Where should I take this big strength?
Only go with flow!

My Midnight Corona Haiku

Oh pandemic time
My Birthdays song sing
By washing my hands

My Corona Change

Now I do what I really want.
Craving chips and coke.

Photo Credit: Jitka Kohlickova

POEM — THE WAY OF LIFE

PAUL D. LOWE (SPAIN)

Life's paths are littered with many variables. We perceive many things about this enigmatic voyage. Just as we become complacent, the volatile compound of fate and human nature has an uncanny habit of reminding us how vulnerable we are.

Many paradoxes exist — the longer we live, the sooner we die; to enjoy peace, we must be aware of others' wars; though born ignorant, we have potential for wisdom.

Throughout the journey, many different phases evolve which – at the time – we may not enjoy or even understand; but we must rest assured, they are a vital part of our life's learning.

Love is the all-powerful emotion that waters us through the aridity of life's desert. It is the difference between merely existing or living life to the full. It is a reason to carry on and grow; life is a gift and like all gifts, it should be treasured.

Loss comes in many forms, each with their own painful legacy. However, we must always remember as surely as the harsh winter of life kills the beautiful summer flowers, so shall new ones grow again in the spring.

We need many things to survive the turbulent waves of life's sea; but above all we need something to sustain us — knowing in our darkest hours we are not alone — we need faith.

Faith is believing that through all our mistakes and selfishness, we will be forgiven — by ourselves and the universe – and progress to live a life of maximum peace, love & happiness.

Paul D. Lowe

Paul has made a remarkable transformation from existing for many years in dark, desperate despair, to now living a really healthy, happy, and fulfilling life.

From an early age, he was in the vice-like clutches of the demon drink and constantly embroiled within a dark cocktail of toxic beliefs, self-hate, and destructive violence.

Paul's purpose is amazingly simple - he is extremely passionate about helping others to find their purpose, have a voice and make a real difference.

Making A Difference — By Helping You Make A Difference!

Contact Paul at www.Paul-Lowe.com

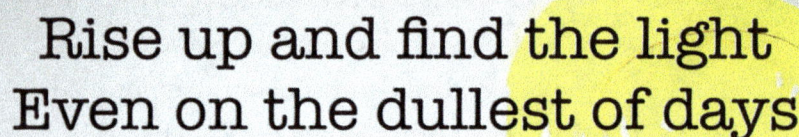

'Sunflowers' by Lorna Reid

POEM — IF IT'S ME

AMANDA HART (SOMERSET, UK)

If it's me,
does it feel like the sun rising to meet the stillness of a new day,
The scent of a forest after rainfall, the smell of jasmine
on a balmy night?
If it's me, does it feel like spring after winter,
as colour brings you alive,
Or the sound of the ocean as it breathes in and out on the shore?

Has your heart sent an invitation on the wind
to entice you to find your beauty?
Without truly knowing why or what that might be?
And when you've been stirred by your own sadness, have you
suppressed it to protect others,
Whilst praying your soul would be rescued, be healed
and set free?

Have you longed for the moments, that bliss in a rainstorm
and hoped that one day it exists?
When your life has become others and no longer just you,
and you long to discover your truth?
How often has lust reared tempting and raw
and you've conquered your hunger and need,
Has logic won over to do just what's right
when your heart cries to throw yourself in?

How often has comfort and norm set your
sails facing south
for what you feel's right,
And while moments of chance give you reason to change,
you have trampled your needs into dust?
Have you sacrificed that which you crave for inside,
but tempts you when you're all alone?
And despite your armour, have you longed for its presence
to set you free, to rebel?

If it's me,
have you heard my voice through the trees respond
when you call out my name,
And felt your heart swell as I enter your soul,
your desires entice you to dance?
If it's me, has my touch on your skin left a mark like the
tenderness of summer rain,
And when you feel my breath, warm near your face,
do you ache for our bodies to meld?

If it's me,
do you long for my strength, to throw caution
into the ocean of chance,
And let yourself go for a while, to be exposed,
naked and true?
If it's me, do you ache for my kiss to remind you
of losing all sense of now,
And to dance in the fire of pleasure and bliss,
and let me wrap you in my sweet ecstasy?

If it's me
do you long for true love that gives all,
the pleasure as well as the pain,
And lets your wildest dreams of adventure
and joy fill you to all that you are?
If it's me, would you walk to the ends of the earth
and give when you've nothing left,
And if it's me, would your heart be content
to watch that sunset and know what you had,
was it all?

Copyright © Amanda Hart, 2020

TEN WAYS TO BRING JOY INTO YOUR DAYS

SABINE KONRATH (GERMANY)

Ten Ways to Bring Joy into Your Days
(for those of us who are home alone right now)

---

1) Start each morning with gratitude. Sounds simple, yes, I know. Just do it. Think of three things you are grateful for right now: small things like your favourite breakfast or the beautiful sunrise, big things like feeling love for your partner. When you are grateful, you radiate positive energy. Life can give you more to be grateful for.

2) Move your body as often as possible: go for a walk in nature (if you live in one of the countries where it is still possible), stretch every 60 minutes if you work at your computer, do online Yoga or a cardio class! Move! Your body will love it!

3) Meditation is another way to feel calm and joyful at the same time. There are many different ways and some great apps, try several until you find your way. A few minutes per day are enough to give you the joy and calm.

4) Meditating not your thing? Try journaling as a way to let your feelings and thoughts out, just write them down, you don't have to read it again, nobody else will see it and it's not literature — so write for 10 minutes and let it out. Sit for a minute and feel into it. Do you already feel lighter? More joyful even?

5) Connect to your family and friends: that's maybe the most important tip right now. Whether you have a chat over the phone, use a messenger, Zoom, whatever — we all need this feeling of being connected to our loved ones.

6) Check in with people you haven't talked to in a while. I sent an email to my friends from university and the responses warmed my heart. I also tried to locate some good friends I haven't talked to for years — I guess they are just one phone call away.

7) Create to feel the joy again. Whether it's writing, knitting, taking pictures, painting — when you use your creativity, whether you enjoy the process or are results oriented, it will lift you up.

8) The same goes for planting — now is the perfect time, if you have a garden or balcony, to plant. You could even put small pots with herbs in the kitchen on the windowsill. There's

nothing like watching something grow, that's giving you the feeling of being alive and joyful.

9) My go-to tip when I feel stuck and blocked is to bake or cook. While the dough is rising, my spirit is rising, too. When I feel low, a meal that reminds me of my childhood will work miracles. It does not have to be complicated, Spaghetti Bolognese will do. Set the table for you as your special guest and enjoy.

10) My favourite way to enjoy life, no matter what, is music. I need my daily dose of music. Whether I listen to my favourite songs, watch a concert or simply put on my dancing shoes for more or less ecstatic dancing — music always lifts my mood, fills me with energy and joy. Dancing is also great for the endorphin levels. I also love to dress up once a week for my dancing session, it changes my mood and it's fun!

You can lose materials.
You can lose fortune.
But Family and Friends
are forever,
And they are one's true
Double Happiness.

Gloria Chin Besthoff
(Greenwich, CT, USA)

LETTER TO THE WORLD FROM MOTHER NATURE

LESLEY MACCULLOCH (SCOTLAND)

Hello my dear, dear friend

I honour you. I honour you right now, wherever you're at, however you feel, I honour you right there. There is nothing you feel that you shouldn't be feeling, and there is nobody you should feel you need to be, other than *you*. I know you've been going through some difficult times in your world lately. I've been watching, and I've been thinking about you a lot so I thought … well, since the world's gone all weird, it won't be that weird for Mother Earth to write you a letter.

You see, I wanted to remind you that I'm here. Not just 'here', as in superficially, or simply existing as a part of your outer world. I'm here. I'm here with you, I'm here for you and I'm here as a part of you.

"What do you mean? How can you be there for me?" I hear you say. *"How can you be part of me?"*

Well, you see, as Mother Nature — or Gaia, as many of you know me as — I am alive. Alive in my splendour and power. I operate at the highest frequency of all, and that is why I can help you.

"I don't know what you mean, or where you're going with this?"

No. That's why I thought I'd write you a letter. Because now is a great time to send a reminder, and explain. But first of all, know I love you. Know I love you more than your human words can ever convey, and that I hold you in that place of love always. Indeed, at my high frequency, I know of no other way. I've been poorly treated by many humans as they work out what it means to operate through love and integrity, to feel humility, express kindness, experience deep gratitude, empower and encourage each other, create trust, and inspire optimism, but my frequency remains high.

It's absolutely fine that you don't know what I mean. Most people don't. When you understand a bit more, we'll be able to work better together. It is through frequency and vibration that I am a part of you, just as you are a part of me. Underneath your fear, your anxiety, your stress, your worry, your anger and frustration, I am with you because we are connected by energy. We are connected by energy because we *are* energy, you and I. We are both energy. We live and exist as part of an energy world. There's nothing else we can be. You are a human; my children, they are trees, they are flowers, they are rivers, they are birds, berries, blossoms, oceans, fields. Yet all of that is secondary to the fact that we are all energy.

You have just not been trained to feel or know how to recognise that energy, nor have you been trained in how to manage, look after and, indeed, heal your own energy.

I'll explain a little bit how it all works, and then I'll tell you how I can help you.

Many people in your human world don't believe about energy because you can't see it. Yes, energy is invisible to the human eye, but energy is also palpable. You may not be able to see it, and you can't touch it, but you can surely *feel* it. The main way you feel energy is through your emotions. Energy tells you how you feel. You will also feel it as an atmosphere, as personal space, as vibes, as throbbing or pulsating, as hot and cold sensations, as tickles, shivers, goose-pimples, bolts, nudges, epiphanies, ideas ... there are so many ways you can feel and experience energy. The point here is to understand that it is *everywhere* and that you *are* it. Your body is made up of energy systems. It is energy that creates life in your body. Energy is what determines the state of your health.

And energy runs on a frequency. Remember the old radios and televisions? Remember how you used to have to fiddle with the knob before you could find a station (the right frequency)? Well, our energy is a lot like that. It tunes in and vibrates at a frequency. I vibrate at a very high frequency and that high frequency radiates love, hope, optimism, inspiration, kindness, gentleness, gratitude. And humans ... well, you *can* vibrate at that beautiful higher vibration, or at least closer to it than you do, but most of the time you don't, because, well, mainly because you don't realise it works like that, but also because you're brought up that life is hard, that you're not good enough, that you can't show your emotions. And these low energy emotions keep you in a low vibration, at a low frequency. And low frequencies keep you in low moods.

But guess what! You *can* vibrate at a higher frequency. And that's why I can help you SO much. Because when you come out into my world, the frequency of my  love and truth has so much power that it lifts you up. I help you to feel better. Even when you come to me at your lowest, you can't pull me down. I love you unconditionally and, as long as you treat me with respect and look after me, I will be there to look after you, to replenish you, and nourish you, and feed your soul. You, alone, can't pull me down. But I, alone, can pull you up.

So, what better thing to do than to surrender to my love and healing.

Many of you do connect with me, through the vehicles of your soul, and we unite, we bond, we lift life together. Many of you bring your dogs, walk by the rivers, reach up to the sun, inhale the fresh oxygen air under the beautiful sky, catch your breath in the fresh breeze. Sit. Many of you just sit, savouring the magic of the continuing and infinite seasonal cycle and the deep truth of life, untouched in its own power, alive and humble, inspiring in its steadiness and certainty.

• • •

Others of you — less than the dog walkers, but still a number of you — come and immerse deeply in the sacredness of my environment, surrendering to the divine natural forces, the waves of energy, the power of the trees, the freshness of the earth, the beauty, the sounds, all the sounds, and the *life*. I am a true miracle, and I embrace the many of you who ground yourselves in my energy *knowing* that it makes you feel better, *needing* the time to be alone with me, honouring your own health and wellness. We connect. We communicate. We share that present moment. You rejuvenate. You recharge. You breathe.

When I speak of you recharging, perhaps I should explain a bit further. It's not just the environment around you that you can see, that replenishes your soul. The earth beneath your feet is *full* of life and abundance, including a network of electrons. Electricity. Remember when you were taught how to change a plug, and you needed the earth wire. Well, what you weren't taught at the same time was that *you* need that earth wire too. Because you, too, are a network of electromagnetic energies that need to be kept charged. You *need* to connect to nature, to earth, to keep yourself healthy physically, spiritually, energetically and emotionally. There is no fuller, better way than connecting with my natural elements through your body, through your food, through your thoughts, beliefs and actions, because I can heal you. Come to me, throw off your shoes, and connect. Soak in the morning dew. Lie on the sand, play in the soil, walk in the leaves, paddle in the rivers, drink out of the pristine streams. BE.

Bring the whole of you into the whole of me. Regularly. I will watch you. I will hold you. I will accept you exactly where you're at. I will never judge you; I will never condemn you; I won't allow you to sit with your anxiety or your fear. And so, you will cleanse. So, you will heal.

But. You must open your world to me. You must ask for my help. You must invite me in. You can sit with me, but you remain your own authority. I cannot assume to help you if you do not ask. Speak to me, ask me things, tell me how you are. Chat. Let's get to know each other. Let's build on the connection we already have. The best thing we can do, for both of us, is become friends.

Of course, you are likely, at first, to feel self conscious, to feel those eyes of judgement upon you as you cast off your shoes, delight in the soil beneath your feet, sit with the tree, be with the tree, unite with the tree. Choose to be done with those judgements. Choose to teach these people. Choose to be the one to show them there are other ways. Be the one to stand up for your own health, and open your heart. Invite them to join you. Nature is truth. My environment will help strip you of your fears. There is nothing more true than that.

And you are blessed enough to be connected to it.

I am alive. I am alive deep under your feet, high above your head, and everywhere in between. I am a system of plenitude, of abundance, of resilience, of unity and creation. I have been here always, and I have no ego, no fear. I stand strong in my faith, my truth and my frequency of love and I can draw you all the way up into a higher vibration. And that's what happens when you come to be with me, when you come to spend time in my presence. I help you to lift your vibration.

And now that you realise that, I will be ready to receive you as you experiment and feel your way forwards and upwards into a place where love is always stronger than fear.

I love you,
with all of my high-vibrational heart.
Mother Earth

Copyright (c) 2020 Lesley MacCulloch

Photos of Nature courtesy of Lesley MacCulloch and Janet Groom from their daily walks

---

Lesley MacCulloch

Lesley is a visionary, a writer and a pioneer of the new age. She works with emerging leaders, individuals and business owners, helping them to embrace their inner authority and reconcile their own unique experience into the new world.

Author of *'Live Your Sunshine – Be Your Light'*, Lesley honours and empowers you into the wholeness of your being as you unlock the truth of your soul and find your own voice.

Lesley also works with modern day organisations that wish to restructure from the traditional hierarchical model, to the more expansive, conscious and higher-frequency heterarchical model, which is based on equal responsibility, collective decision-making, and self and group empowerment.

Contact Lesley at www.lesleymacculloch.com

SURVIVAL TOOLS

ANGELA HECK (SWITZERLAND)

**Your personal toolbox
to surviving
the 'Tumbler Time'**

Sometimes life feels like someone external has put you in a tumble dryer and pressed the start button.

Usually these things happen in each and everyone's personal world. But now, this has changed, we are all in together — some more, some less — but all being thrown around, upside down and inside out.

I would like to offer you some ideas on how to deal with this special time in particular, but also with moments like this in the future.

Tool 1: HOW TO IGNORE THE NEWS

How things are different to what they were 100 years ago…

We've now got social media and news which spreads immediately across the world in seconds.

Bearing this in mind, we come directly to tool number one.

 Stop reading the news!

It is easily said but not easily done, so this is how I learned to stop reading the news…

I started to just read the news titles:

' The cheapest and worst paper..'
' Then the second one…' and so, on

While reading the titles you will realise that the BIG thing is not as big as they say. You will start to feel the not existing energy behind the title, and you will lose the urge to read or listen to everything.

Artwork - 'The Whale and the Pussycat went to Sea' by Claudia España and Benjaphon Khidhathong

Do this and you will start to feel and recognise what you need to read and what is supporting you, rather than those news articles which just suck energy from you and feed the fear.

Tool 2: CONNECT WITHIN YOURSELF DEEPLY AND TRULY

Make sure that you breathe deep into your feet and allow your roots to grow and spread out deep into the earth.

STEP 1: Sit down comfortably — on a chair, on the floor, whatever works for you.
STEP 2: Breathe consciously and when inhaling, visualise the air going all the way to your feet. Repeat 3-4 times.
STEP 3: Imagine that colourful roots are growing from your feet, digging their way into the soil, connecting you with Mother Earth. Feel your roots grow deeper and deeper, and take whatever colour is ready to be the colours of the roots.
STEP 4: Notice how your mind is calming down and sense your body from the top of your head, to the very tips of your fingers and toes.
STEP 5: Ask your Intuition, where do you live? How can I know for certain it's you - the voice of love - and not fear?
STEP 6: Where in your body did you feel a response? Visualise marking this place with your favourite colour or perhaps a shape, like a heart or a star - make sure you remember!

Repeat this 2-3 times daily for a few weeks. Allowing the connection to become stronger and natural. If you then go grocery shopping, for example, and you can feel the vibration and stress surrounding you, you just need to think '*roots* and you feel the connection and strength of Mother Earth.

Tool 3: STAY TRUE TO YOUR HEART

This is the most natural wisdom and connection within us, which we somehow lost.

Knowledge is a lot more than what we learn in school and keep in our brain. We are body, mind and soul and all three have a different knowledge. The best is to combine all three tools, with the knowledge we carry in our heart — *your heart knows the way*. Therefore you carry the strength and wisdom within you.

 Your heart knows the way

Now, you might ask yourself how to connect with your heart. This is as easy as it can be.

Put a hand on your heart and listen within you what *answer* you get. This can be a voice you hear or a feeling you get.

No one of the three tools is better than the other one. Try all of them or choose the first one which works the easiest for you — then try out all of them over time. Do this and you find which one of the tools is best to use in a specific situation.

Angela Heck

Angela is a Psychic Life Coach for women who have lost themselves in business and she supports them to find their own "gut knowledge".

Angela grew up in the same Swiss village as the writer Johanna Spyri, the author of *Heidi*, where she enjoyed 'a picture book childhood'.

Her greatest wish is that in companies and schools it becomes even more a matter of course that "gut knowledge" gets is empowerment as "brain knowledge".

Contact Angela at www.angelaheck.com

Happy Safari
Jane Young
(Kent, UK)

FROM BUSY TO BEING

EMMA MANYWEATHERS (KENT, UK)

During week two of isolation I was vigorously scarifying the earth preparing to seed the ten-foot circle of dead lawn where the trampoline used to live. This was task five on a list of twenty something more substantial jobs to get done during these peculiar times. I was working up quite a sweat given how unfit I had become recently. In my mind I heard my late grandmothers voice softly questioning me, "Why can't you just be?" I remembered that as a child I would rarely sit idle for long. Patiently she would roll her eyes, put down her knitting and humour me, "you will probably learn cack handed, I'm left-handed and you're not!", "I don't care, I just want to learn how to knit", I implored… and I did. I always had to be up to my eyeballs in glitter and glue, writing stories, or pottering in the garden creating dreadful rose petal perfume. The perfume was intended to earn my fortune, whisking me away from the council estate I was raised on, funding the castle I was actually supposed to live in at eight years old. Not much has changed. Recently, I saw an advert on the TV for a beautiful paradise holiday, you know the type, white sandy beaches for miles and nothing to do except order cocktails. My husband viewed it longingly, he commented how lovely that would be, especially right now. I smiled agreeably, knowing it was my idea of torture unless I had a craft project and a stack of books beside me. I pondered; how could people just lay there rotating in the sun all day? I said nothing. I realised I have never been able to just be.

 There is a TIME to DO. There is a TIME to BE. Sometimes we need to step back to move forward.
— *Janet Groom*

My childhood and adolescent years had plenty of challenges. I spent my teenage years thinking I must achieve a career with guaranteed income, enough to facilitate a comfortable country home for my six children I was yet to create, along with numerous cocker spaniels and a substantial vegetable garden. The highest school grades I achieved were in Art and English. I was happiest during those lessons and frequently regretted dropping textiles as a subject. I chose the subjects I thought would lead me to a steady and guaranteed income, a stability I'd lacked. My grades indicated some degree of creative skill, but I chose to ignore the signs even though I felt happiest during those lessons. I didn't recognise that maybe the universe was telling me something, instead I ignored what made me happy and chose what I thought was right.

I would have liked a creative career but considered it too much of a gamble unless you were utterly brilliant. I felt average, how could I be brilliant? I would, and still do, blush if praised for an achievement, in true British style I self-sabotage a compliment sent my way. So, whilst raising my own family, blessed with four children and one cocker spaniel, I spent 25 years working with visually impaired children, fitting this in around my family life and school runs. I enjoyed it, it was rewarding, but I reached my late 30's and desired a change. I completed two degrees whilst going through a divorce, falling in love and dealing with a hefty smattering of trauma.

One of the degrees qualified me as an occupational therapist and I switched to working in mental health services. A knowing soul once told me that many people who experience poor mental health or have supported family members through it, gravitate to roles in this field. I have experienced periods of my life that have been challenging. 4am has often greeted me with varying degrees of heart racing panic and a raging solar plexus, waiting for the sounds from the outside to indicate the world is awake, meaning it was acceptable for me to go and put the kettle on without anyone realising anything was wrong. I know how it feels to lay in bed staring at the ceiling, listening to audio books, guided meditations, soaking up positive thinking advice from strangers across the pond, some days wanting to pull the duvet back over me and just stay there, not that you can when you have responsibilities. Dash of lipstick, big smile and nobody knew of the restless soul behind the façade. Just keep going, keep achieving, plough on through the difficult times by keeping busy.

There are aspects of working in mental health that I love; working with people, listening to their narratives and trying to find ways to support them to recover from a troubled mind. What is that person's thing? Their *raison d'être*, their protective factor. I genuinely care. However, I recognise that I am an empath, and one of the pitfalls of being an empath is that you suck up people's energies and need to look after yourself too. Over time I found I was waking up at 4am again. This time my heart wasn't galloping, it was more a low volume alarm bell. It wasn't past traumas or my husband's experience of cancer or the wellbeing of my children. I was generally unsettled. I recognised the balance of family life and working was uneven. My family and household chores were neglected but I continued to reconcile these thoughts that I was doing the right thing by helping others whilst paying the bills. I had an inkling that something had to give, I just couldn't work out how, so I kept going.

Then one morning my husband received a letter from the NHS. It advised that he must isolate for twelve weeks due to the *global pandemic*, he is considered one of the vulnerable. He began reading it aloud "OK! Let's talk about it tonight" I said as I dashed out the door. I yelled "I love you, have a good day", to my still rousing children and for the umpteenth time in my life I didn't know which way to turn. As I drove through the country lanes thoughts raced with an internal argument. Should I move out of the family home to reduce the risk of me passing this dreaded virus on to him or the children? Yet, they need their wife and mother, surely everything will fall apart without me around? But I'm a keyworker, I am meant to care for service users, it's my duty. What about the amazing team I work with? Although, I *had* nearly lost my husband two years ago, for us the cancer is a ticking time bomb and had already caused us to re-evaluate life once before. What it boiled down to was pride — I've always done everything, and this time I couldn't.

'Butterfly' by Lorna Reid (Northern Ireland)

The global pandemic has been altering our lives in more ways than expected. My husband asked me to leave my job and stay at home with the family, "we will figure something out once this passes, this is out of our control". Even though the exhausted little angel on my shoulder was telling me it was the right thing to do, to just let go this time and let things unfold without controlling everything, of course I had to ruminate and catastrophise every eventuality. After a few sleepless nights I agreed. For a while, I cringed every time I heard the words NHS heroes, or when I stood on my doorstep clapping in gratitude to those that chose to keep going or simply had no choice. I felt like a failure, a deserter. Ultimately, the global pandemic and cancer forced a change that I probably wouldn't have otherwise made. I left my job, grateful that I had the option but feeling an immense sense of failure. I couldn't do it all.

 Then, slowly I started to notice the blessings.

I don't detract or underestimate the devastation and uncertainty this time has caused for many. I am worried for everyone's wellbeing, the bills and so on, I miss my family and friends, but something has shifted. I've noticed I am drifting off to sleep at night, no meditation or self-medication, no essential oils wafting around my room. I am awaking to the sound of birdsong outside my window: robins, sparrows and blue tits, not seagulls the size of pterodactyls; no rattle of trains or nearby delivery lorries, just a beautiful dawn chorus. No racing heart at 4am, just lying in bed next to my beloved husband in the still small hours of the morning enjoying the peace, albeit intermittent snoring but a deep sense of gratitude. He, the one, is still beside me, snoring and all. No toxic rumination, only gratitude for the gardening I might do today, wondering what magical gift of nature has grown in my greenhouse overnight. Slowly, the stash of wool overflowing the cupboard is gradually turning into blankets and cardigans, alleviating the anxiety that disorder bestows me, simultaneously enjoying the thrill of rummaging through a wool stash that only a fellow crafter can truly appreciate. The screenshots in my phone of nutritious meals I will make one day are actually being created and devoured at a reasonable time. I no longer throw something together late evening after a long commute feeling like a lousy wife and mother.

I have time to read the pile of books that I've brought on day trips that adorned my shelves seemingly never to be read. I can research things on the internet that I want to, not need to for the sake of getting degrees, I am reading the things that inspire me. I have looked through photographs with the horrid realisation that I barely remember certain events because I have been ridiculously busy and burnt out. I was there in body, the photographs evidence it, but I was not present. I recognised that when my son is upstairs, I haven't adjusted to the sound of his deep voice and how it catches me off guard wondering who that man is upstairs talking! I can now listen to my youngest child tell a story that shamefully I previously would have been squirming thinking 'When is this going to end as I really need to get some washing in the machine, make the lunch boxes or study?' I can reflect on the last few years and how they have been utter chaos in the pursuit of doing the right thing, I thought it was important to keep busy, my priorities were all wrong.

I am no longer waking at 4am but closer to five and I'll take that because it turns out 5am is a good time to walk to the beach with my youngest daughter and watch the sunrise whilst listening to her chatter incessantly. When I awake early, I can put the kettle on as it doesn't matter if I make a little noise, the rest of the house can roll over and go back to sleep. There are no deadlines right now. I have realised that a conventional sleep and work pattern doesn't suit me. 5:30am is a good time for me to write and get into a flow, the house is peaceful at this hour. I love people watching, I can sit at my desk typing, looking out through the gaps in the blinds observing the street gradually waking up. Until now I never knew that my neighbour went for a run at 6am, maybe she didn't before, maybe this gift of time has granted her exercise.

I have wanted to write something other than an academic piece or a shopping list for many years and therefore I have achieved something in so much that you are reading this, something I've wanted since childhood.

The current circumstances have challenged long held beliefs about myself, I am listening to my inner voice at last. Actually, I am not someone who thrives on keeping busy, the next venture, the next challenge, ultimately it was to mine and my family's detriment. I don't thrive on pressure; I thrive being around my family and nature. I certainly thrive on learning but I also I thrive on creating, or immersed in the creative, inspirational or spiritual.

Naturally, I want the global pandemic and many of its impacts to pass. But on reflection, this slower pace of life suits me better and I am grateful for the time to realise this. I will return to work when it is safe to do so but for now things are uncertain, so I am using the time productively, slowly ticking off the to — do lists that never got done whilst I was at university or working, but also thinking of ways to create a better normality. I know I need the balance of doing what I love career wise but also having a quality family life whilst making the time to be creative and do the things I enjoy. Even though I've had chapters of my life where I've thought I've been cursed, it turns out I am blessed, not only with family and company right now, but time to breathe, to think, somehow things seem simpler. If we don't use this period of time to re-evaluate now, then when? Most importantly I have learned that the world is not going to implode if I rest. Such irony that during a hellish time I can be most at peace.

 It would appear I can just *BE* after all.

'Just BEE' by Lorna Reid (Northern Ireland)

Raising Your Vibe

Here's some ideas to try and focus on if ever you find your mood dipping. Doing any one of these things will help you to get in flow, 'in the zone', and ultimately lift your spirits.
Maybe try creating your own A-Z and do at least one each day

Today I am going to focus on...

A - Animals
B - Breath
C - Crystals
D - Dance
E - Exercise
F - Focusing
G - Gratitude
H - Healing
I - Imagining
J - Journaling
K - Kinship
L - Laughing
M - Mindfulness

N - Nature
O - Optimism
P - Painting
Q - Qigong
R - Reading
S - Singing
T - Theta
U - Unicorns
V - Vortex
W - Writing
X - Xenodochy
Y - Yellow
Z - Zestiness

Sharon Lynn - The Entrepreneurial Lightworker
& Mystic Mouse Publishing

ACKNOWLEDGMENTS

It is with a grateful heart I would like to personally thank everyone who contributed, and the following people for their support in helping me to turn all the words and images into a book.

To our editing team — **Ellen Mullen** with her great eye for detail, and **Eileen Reid** for proofreading.

A huge thank you to **Sue Allsworth** for your endless belief in me, the project and your support to create the amazing promotional video and much more.

To my dear husband, **Mark**, who is so tolerant of me and my grand ideas.

To all the artists/photographers for their artwork which has been credited throughout the book. Other images used are courtesy of Pixabay.com.

Finally, to you, **Dear Reader**, for buying this book. May you enjoy it and I hope it will UPLIFT you, and please tell your friends to grab a copy too.

THANK YOU & FREE GIFTS FOR YOU

Click here to claim your FREE gifts for purchasing the book - courses, handouts, free discovery sessions and more…
www.janetgroom.com/upliftbookfreebies/

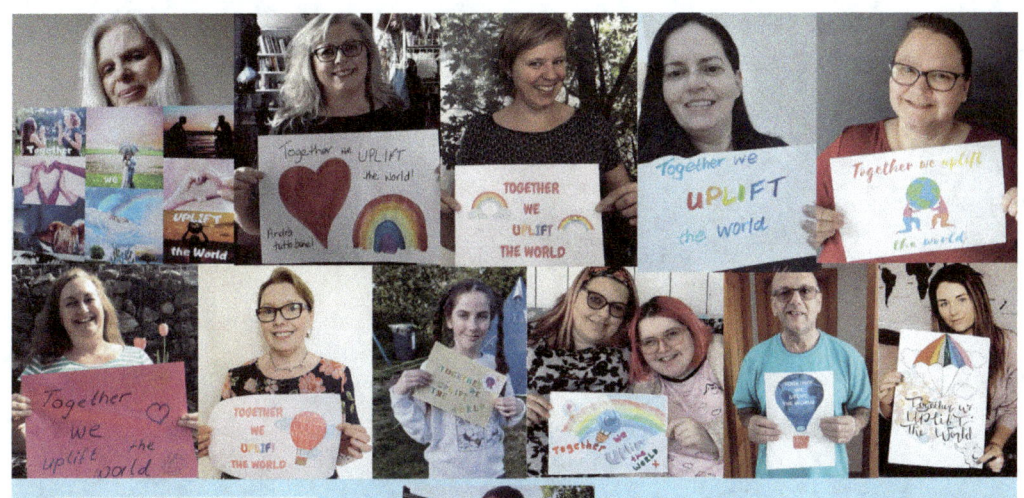

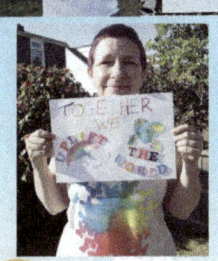

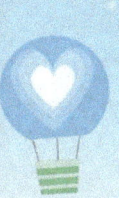

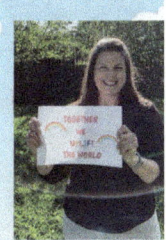

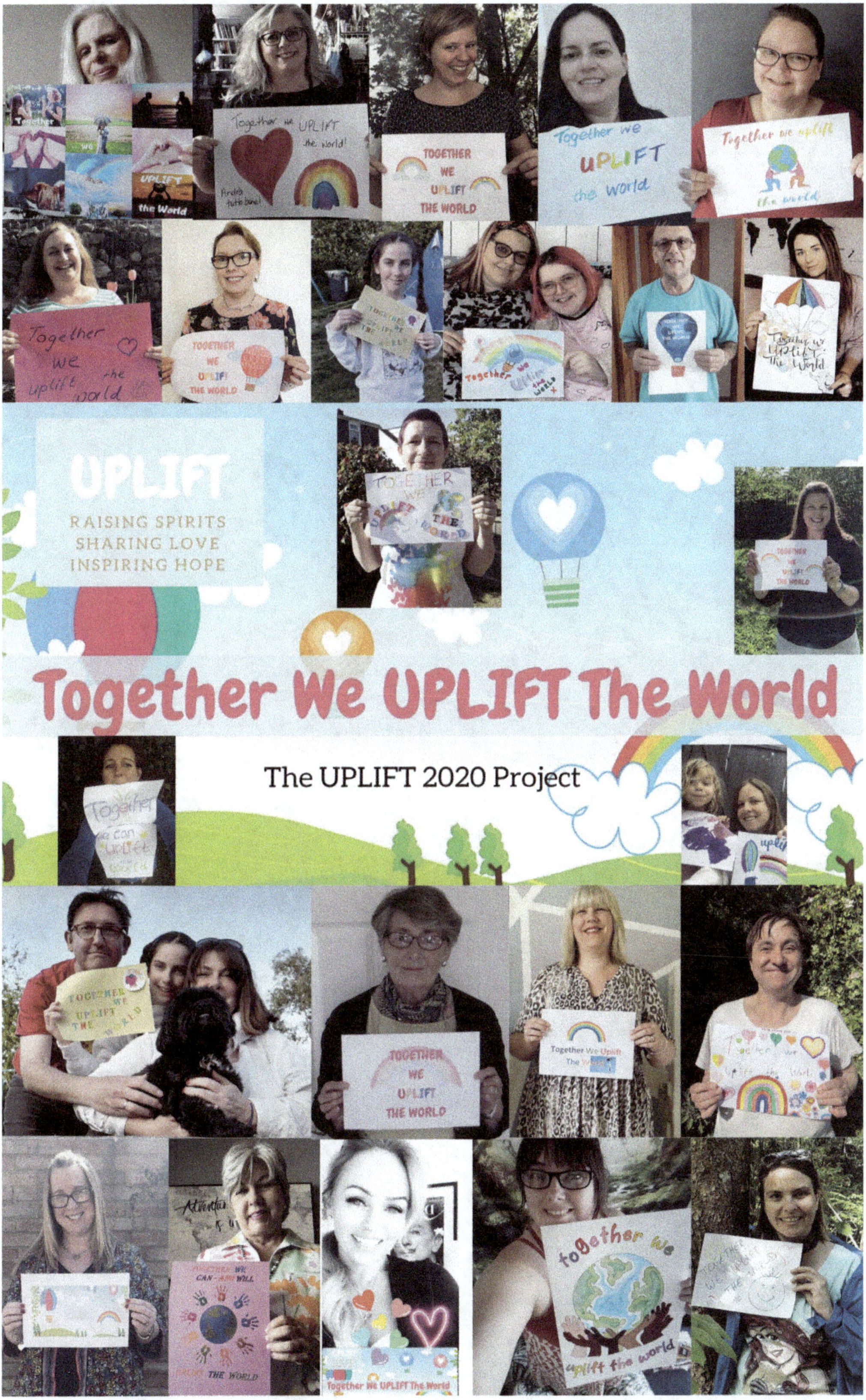
UPLIFT
RAISING SPIRITS
SHARING LOVE
INSPIRING HOPE
Together We UPLIFT The World
The UPLIFT 2020 Project

CONTRIBUTORS

Caroline Palmy (Author, Speaker and Heart Flow Healer), Switzerland www.carolinepalmy.com

Susanne Mueller (Executive Coach, Author, Blogger and Podcaster) New York, USA www.susannemueller.biz

Angela Brittain (Author, Speaker and Certified Dream Builder Coach) Texas, USA www.angelabrittainllc.com

Amanda Hart (Intuitive Consultant & Author) Somerset, UK www.amanda-hart.co.uk

Paul D. Lowe (Author, Podcaster & Game-changing Coach) Spain www.Paul-Lowe.com

Sue Allsworth (Founder of Authentic Smile & Journal Journey Coaching) Kent, UK www.authenticsmile.com

Angela Heck (Psychic Life Coach) Switzerland
www.angelaheck.com

Jane Scanlan (Confidence Coach, Author) Bournemouth, UK
www.cherishtransformupgrade.com

Kavitha Chahel (Founder of Compassionism) Global Citizen
www.compassionism.com

James Moffat (Coach, Speaker & Storyteller) Switzerland
www.facebook.com/jamesmoffat3

Lesley MacCulloch (Coach & Writer) Scotland
www.lesleymacculloch.com

Sharon Lynn (The Entrepreneurial Lightworker & Publisher) Kent, UK www.mysticmouse-publishing.com/

Helen Ree (Photographer) Switzerland www.helenree.com

Pete Stanley (Photographer) Kent, UK
www.petesphotography.net

Karin Hagelin (Life Crisis Coach) Switzerland
www.karinhagelin.ch

Rhiannon Archard (Illustrator and Community Artist) Kent, UK
www.rhiannonarchard.co.uk

Mojca Fo (Artist) Ljubljana, Slovenia
www.fo.si

Emma Devereux (Artist) Kent, UK
www.facebook.com/busy.bee.artwork.2020/

Lisa Newman - Kent, UK
Jenny Luddington - Kent, UK
Ellie J. Hart - UK
Hayley Kennett - Kent, UK
Archie Reynolds - Kent, UK
Claudia España - Kent UK
Benjaphon Khidhathong - Kent, UK
Vikki Hills - Kent, UK
Catman (Artist) - Kent, UK
April Austen - Kent, UK
Ella Austen - Kent, UK
Gloria Chin Besthoff - Greenwich, CT, USA
Sarah Richards - Leeds, UK
Lorna Reid - Northern Ireland
Sabrine Konrath - Germany
Lisa Hall - Kent, UK
Jeanne Elin - Bristol, UK
Johnny, Lydia & Harriet Homer - Kent, UK
Nicky Thompson - Kent, UK
Eileen Reid - Northern Ireland
Jitka Kohlickova - Kent, UK
Emma Manyweathers - Kent, UK
Jane Young - Kent, UK

JOIN THE THE UPLIFT 2020 PROJECT

Join the UPLIFT Hub group on Facebook
https://www.facebook.com/groups/UPLIFTHub/

SUBSCRIBE and follow our UPLIFT HUB YouTube Channel
https://www.youtube.com/
channel/UCFjpzip0fm9R23EzALc8Nvg

DONATIONS TO SUPPORT
NHSCharitiesTogether.co.uk * Mind.org.uk * Porchlight.org.uk
www.justgiving.com/crowdfunding/uplift-2020

FREE GIFTS FOR YOU
Click here to claim your FREE gifts for purchasing the book - courses, handouts, free discovery sessions and more…
www.janetgroom.com/upliftbookfreebies/

JANET GROOM - FOUNDER OF THE UPLIFT 2020 PROJECT

Janet Groom is a Transformational Life Coach, Author, Trainer, Speaker and Book Coach/Publisher. She considers herself to be a multi-faceted diamond in the rough with a heart of gold.

At the beginning of the global pandemic, she was moved to create something to support people and the idea for the UPLIFT Book was born, which led to the formation of The UPLIFT 2020 Project.

Find out more about Janet at www.janetgroom.com

Books by Janet Groom

Find out about Janet's other books (fiction and non-fiction) at
www.janetgroom.com/my-books

Fiction:
'The Naked Knitting Club — Casting On'

Non-Fiction:
'Write to Heal'
'Live the Rainbow'

ALP HOUSE PUBLISHING

ALP House Publishing is an Independent Publishing company offering hybrid publishing services to authors who wish to inspire, motivate and share words of wisdom into the world.

For more information about the books published by ALP House Publishing, and their publishing services, please visit the website

www.alphousepublishing.com

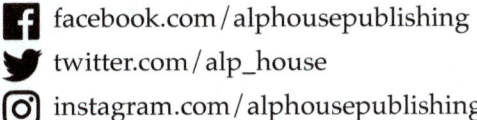

facebook.com/alphousepublishing
twitter.com/alp_house
instagram.com/alphousepublishing

www.ingramcontent.com/pod-product-compliance
Lightning Source LLC
LaVergne TN
LVHW021947060526
838200LV00043B/1952